FAMOUS IDAHOANS

By Richard J. Beck

Moscow, Idaho

1989

To: Doug & Jan

Dick Beck

First edition. Printed by Williams Printing, Boise, Idaho 83702.

Cover artwork and selected sketches by Victoria Brooks-Miller.

ISBN: 0-9623034-0-2

Library of Congress Catalog Card Number: 89-91727

DEDICATION

To my parents, Frank and Mary Beck, for their enduring faith, love, and good example, and to all the famous Idahoans listed herein.

- R.J.B.

i

PREFACE

Idaho is many things. It is nature's wonderland with an abundance of rugged mountains, fertile valleys, wandering rivers, primitive forests, alpine lakes, rolling prairies, streams, canyons and deserts.

Idaho covers 82,413 square miles and ranks 13th in size among the states. It is twice the size of Delaware, New Jersey, New Hampshire, Rhode Island, Vermont and Massachusetts combined and larger than Austria, Belgium, Denmark and Switzerland combined. Its mean elevation is 5,000 ft. and it is said that if Idaho were flattened out it would be bigger than the State of Texas.

Its highest point is Mt. Borah at 12,662 feet and the lowest is on the Snake River at 710 feet above sea level. Our only seaport is Lewiston at 747 feet elevation. The Snake River, which runs through Idaho, is 1,036 miles long and ranks sixth among the nation's rivers.

Hell's Canyon is the deepest gorge in the US and Shoshone Falls is higher than Niagara Falls. Astronauts trained at the Craters of the Moon before going to the moon because it was so much like the moon's surface. Attempts are underway to make it Idaho's first national park.

Idaho is famous for its potatoes but it should also be famous for its people and that's what this book is all about. I have chosen to write brief sketches of one hundred people, living or dead, with an Idaho connection, who have achieved a degree of fame and who were born, raised, retired or died in Idaho. Whether or not they considered Idaho their home - they all lived here and had an Idaho connection. I am not a professional historian and make no judgement as to their historical importance. As we all know fame is fleeting and some of these people may no longer be household words but their contribution is nevertheless important. These biographies run the gamut of actors and athletes, business people, educators, inventors, medical and military people, religious, teachers and writers, rich and poor, the very educated and the uneducated.

We have watched them on stage, screen, and television. We have listened to their music and speeches, read their poems and stories, crossed their bridges, used their inventions, their airplanes and many other products.

We have benefited from their inventions, such as teflon, cortisone and television; marvelled at the dams they built; and at their leadership.

The list of one hundred is admittedly subjective. Someone else might select a different one hundred people. Some of "your names" probably appear in the addenda list.

Before I came to Idaho in 1957 or knew there was an Idaho connection, I enjoyed the stories of Hemingway, the Tarzan books, the music of Roger Williams, and the acting of Lana Turner and Marjorie Reynolds in the movies. Pappy Boyington was a hero to me in World War II and Weyerhaeuser was a well-known name in St. Paul where I was raised. Carol Ryrie Brink lived just six blocks away in her later life, though I didn't know it then. As a child I played with an erector set invented by A.C. Gilbert, dreamed of visiting Sun Valley, admired the sculptures on Mt. Rushmore, and read about Senator William Borah, the Lion of Idaho.

The biographical information is limited but sources of additional information are listed in the back. Suggestions for additional names are welcome as is additional pertinent biographical information. UI in the text refers to the University of Idaho.

I wish to express my sincere appreciation to Mrs. Karen Davis for typing and re-typing all of this, and Keith Peterson for his advice and encouragement.

And at this time I wish to acknowledge and thank Victoria Brooks-Miller for the cover design and sketches; for proof-reading -- Gail Eckwright, Donna Hanson, and J. Muriel Saul. All are from the UI Library.

Photos of the biographees were obtained from many sources. However, special thanks are due Lynda Irons of The Statesman (Boise) and Sean Means of The Idahonian (Moscow); from UI, Kathy Graham (Alumni Office), Leo Ames (News Bureau), Terry Abraham and Lois Ackaret (Library Special Collections), and Stephen Lyons (Idaho, the University magazine) as well as Mary Reed (LCHS), Tom Trusky (BSU), Paul Krause (LCSC), Elizabeth Jaycox (ISHS), and Phyllis Collins and Barry Kough (LMT).

Richard J. Beck

TABLE OF CONTENTS

AGEE, William M.   **1938-**   **Boise**

Boise-born Morrison Knudsen Chief Executive Officer, William Agee, "worked for peanuts, uh cookies," according to a write up on him in <u>USA Today</u> (September 2, 1988):

> Agee's first job put him in the chips--chocolate chips, that is. The man who
> gained notoriety for losing his job at Bendix Corporation after leading an
> unsuccessful takeover of Martin Marietta Corporation in 1982 started out
> picking dandelions from his neighbors' lawns. His pay: chocolate chip cookies.
> For his father, Agee mowed lawns, washed windows and carried out clinkers
> - the rock-like chunks that develop in coal furnaces. He was paid $70 a month
> but gave two-thirds "to my mother for board and room."
>
> Agee, 50, is now chairman and chief executive of Morrison Knudsen Corporation
> in his hometown of Boise, Idaho. Early jobs taught him a lot about money -
> and banks. "I learned what N.S.F. meant - non sufficient funds."

Agee was born January 5, 1938 in Boise. He attended Stanford University from 1956-57, received an A.A. degree from Boise Junior College in 1958, a B.S., with high honors, from UI in 1960 and an M.B.A. from Harvard in 1963.

He held various positions with Boise Cascade Corporation from 1963-72 when he joined the Bendix Corporation. He served as President and CEO of Bendix from 1977-83.

Upon his return to Idaho as M-K CEO in August 1988, Agee told a news conference his goal is simple:

> Return the company to profitability. People don't like to see red numbers
> (losses). I like to under-promise and over-perform. Morrison Knudsen is
> a world class company with world class growth potential. My job is to ensure
> that we maintain the financial muscle and clear strategic thinking to realize
> that potential. -<u>Lewiston Tribune</u> , August 6, 1988.

Morrison Knudsen (M-K) has about 15,000 employees worldwide and has revenue about $2 billion in engineering, construction and ship building and is among the nations largest contract mining organizations.

Albertson, Joseph A.   **1906-**   **Boise**

"In good times or bad people have to eat, so I figure it's a good business." With that Joe Albertson, owner of one of the country's largest grocery chains explained why he went into the grocery business. Albertson's Inc. is in the news a lot but Joe Albertson is a very "private person" and some of this biographical information is from what is claimed to be the very first interview he ever granted and which appeared in the Supermarket News, New York, N.Y. August 18, 1969. The article begins:

> "I've made a hell of a lot of mistakes, but I haven't made enough to be fatal."
> J.A. Albertson, chairman of the board and chief executive officer of Albertson's
> Inc. chuckles heartily. He laughs often and smiles even more. "I enjoy life to the
> fullest ... I like to work, to be occupied. I like to salt and pepper enough pleasure
> between work to get more out of life." He looks up and adds with a grin that trims years
> from his age. "I think I'm normal in that respect."

Albertson was born October 17, 1906 in Yukon, Oklahoma, the son of a horticulturist and farmer. The family moved to Idaho in 1909 when Joe was three and homesteaded in the sagebrush six miles west of Caldwell. That first interview stated "Joe Albertson looks like a gruff, burly, ramrod (working boss of a cattle spread), who has gotten a little paunchy from too much ledger work. The picture is not too far fetched, because he grew up pitching and bailing hay, bucking wheat sacks, and digging irrigation ditches."

Albertson started clerking at Safeway in 1927 and quit April 1, 1939 after having risen through the ranks to supervise sixteen stores out of Ogden, Utah. He had decided to go into business for himself, and the first Albertson's store was opened July 21, 1939 at 7 a.m. at 16th and State Streets in Boise. It took every cent he had saved and all he could borrow ($5,000). That store was open 7 a.m. to midnight and was one of the most modern supermarkets in the country with its own bakery, magazine racks, a popcorn machine, and "our own ice cream. I didn't go to bed for two days before we opened ... because nobody knew how to make ice cream and I had to stay up to do it." That opening touched off a six months price war that ended in December when Albertson declared a truce. That year Albertson's made a profit of $9,711 while its competitors lost money. In 1982 that first stored was closed and Joe Albertson himself, at age 75, cut the ribbon for the new store (no. 415 in the Albertson chain) across the street, about 50 yards north of the original, at 16th and Washington. He said then his strategy from the beginning was to "fight like hell" to protect his investment and overcome the competition from Safeway, his former employer. He said determination and top-notch employees are the key to building a successful business. In 1988 Albertson's ranked sixth in sales with over 450 stores in seventeen states.

"It's Joe Albertson's supermarket, but the produce department is mine."

ALEXANDER, Moses   1853-1932   Boise

When the polls closed and the votes were counted November 3, 1914, Moses Alexander had been elected Governor of Idaho, the first man of the Jewish faith to be elected governor in the United States. He was born in Bavaria, in Southern Germany, November 13, 1853, the youngest of eight children. His father died shortly thereafter and the children had to work to support their invalid mother. Rafe Gibbs writes about Alexander in <u>Beckoning the Bold</u>:

> There was little opportunity for schooling, but somehow Alexander learned Latin well, because his most treasured possession was a prize received for scholarly achievement in the language -- a Latin book inscribed by the King of Bavaria.
> At 14, Alexander came to America, living for awhile with two sisters in NYC, then moving to Chillicothe, MO., to work as a janitor in a clothing store operated by a cousin.

In Chillicothe he learned to speak and read English and studied American history, especially the Constitution. Alexander became a Democrat, and Mason; acquired a wife (Helena) and four children. At 21 he became a partner in a clothing store and began his political career. He was elected to the City Council in 1886 and became mayor in 1887. Although things were going well in Missouri he left in 1891 for the gold mines of Alaska but stopped at Pocatello along the way, liked what he saw, and bought some land. Continuing on to Boise he established a clothing store there on July 14, 1891. The business prospered and he soon opened stores in Twin Falls, Burley and Blackfoot and became a well-known Idaho merchant. David Crowder writes of Alexander in <u>Tales of Eastern Idaho</u>:

> Soon Alexander entered Idaho's political scene. He was elected mayor of Boise in 1897 and again in 1901. He ran unsuccessfully for governor on the Democratic ticket in 1908. In 1914 he was a candidate for governor again. This time he was successful. He was re-elected in 1916. He was Idaho's governor when great national and international issues were being debated, chiefly prohibition and World War I.

Alexander was a hard campaigner and a good speaker on the street corner and in the farm fields, and Idahoans loved his style. He died January 4, 1934 in Boise, age 78. The original Alexander's Men's Store building still stands on the corner of 9th and Idaho Streets in Boise. His Queen Anne style home on the corner of Third and State Streets, built in 1897 now houses the Commission on the Arts.

ANDRUS, Cecil Dale   **1931-**   **Boise**

President Jimmy Carter said when he announced Andrus' nomination as U.S. Secretary of the Interior on December 18, 1976: "I believe this is the only Cabinet post where I never considered any other person for the position. I've known whom I wanted from the beginning." Carter called Andrus an "environmental pragmatist," a man who makes decisions on environmental issues with an awareness of their economic impact.

Andrus was born August 25, 1931 in Hood River, Oregon and spent his boyhood on a farm in logging country, where his father was a saw mill operator. His first jobs were in the forests and lumber mills of northern Oregon, where he spent a good deal of time hunting, fishing and camping. Andrus attended Oregon State University, 1948-49, and served in the U.S. Navy from 1951-55, the last three years in the Pacific Theater, and was discharged with the rank of aviation electronic technician, second class. Andrus then went to work for TruCut Lumber in Orofino where he became production manager.

Current Biography (1977) says:

> In 1961 Andrus made an auspicious entry into politics, when he was elected for a two-year
> term to the Idaho State Senate from the sixth district, representing Clearwater County.
> He captured for the Democrats a seat that had been Republican for twelve years and became
> the youngest state senator in Idaho history, at age 29. Elected for a second term,
> he served until 1966. As a state senator, Andrus demonstrated a sense of fiscal responsibility
> and worked for legislation in such areas as education, conservation, social services,
> agriculture and business.

He served in the State Senate from 1961-66, and 1969-70. In 1970 he was elected governor, the first Democratic governor in Idaho in 24 years. He served as Governor of Idaho from 1971-77 and U.S. Secretary of the Interior from 1977-81. In 1976 he served as chairman of the National Governor's Conference and in 1980 was named Conservationist of the Year by the National Wildlife Association. In 1986 he was re-elected to the "best job in the world," Governor of Idaho. He was chosen in a 1987 Idaho Statesman poll as the "most powerful person in the state." Others in the top ten were industrialist J.R. Simplot, U.S. Senator James McClure, Idaho State Senate President Pro Tem James Risch, Boise Cascade CEO John Fery, businessman Duane Hagadone, Idaho House Speaker Tom Boyd, U.S. Senator Steve Symms, Albertson's founder Joe Albertson, and U.S. Representative Larry Craig. Andrus received an honorary degree from UI in 1976.

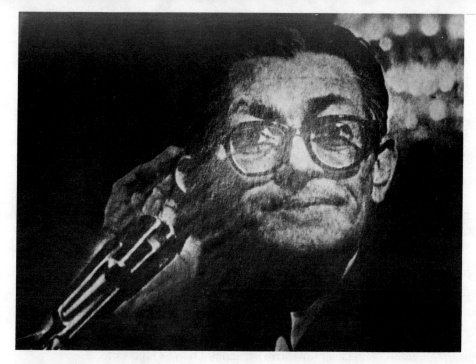

ANGLETON, James J.   **1917-87**   **Boise**

"The Spy Who Came into the Heat" was the headline <u>Time</u> magazine used in its story on Boise-born CIA counterintelligence genius James J. Angleton in its January 6, 1975 issue. The <u>Newsweek</u> issue of the same date said:

> If John Le Carre and Graham Greene had collaborated on a superspy, the result might have been James Jesus Angleton, 57, the head of the Central Intelligence Agency's Counterintelligence Department and, until his abrupt resignation last week, one of its most powerful and least known men. To a former colleague, Angleton was a "spook's spook, the complete secret agent, a man completely engrossed, and I think, completely obsessed with the tactics of espionage." ...Like other CIA men of his generation, Angleton was of the old school, boyhood in Italy, prep school in England, poetry and soccer at Yale. He had barely enrolled in Harvard Law School, when Pearl Harbor was bombed, plunging the U.S. into war and Angleton into the Office of Strategic Services, the precursor of the CIA.

Angleton was born December 9, 1917 in Boise, the son of James Hugh Angleton, a businessman with foreign connections. Young Angleton spent his boyhood in Italy, attended prep school in England and went to Yale (class of 1941) where he edited the <u>Furioso</u> literary magazine publishing Ezra Pound, T.S. Eliot, etc.

After two years in Harvard Law School he followed his father, who had become a Lt. Col. in the OSS, into that agency. Immediately after WWII he worked for a US intelligence operation in Italy that helped pro-American politicians win election over leftist opponents and joined the CIA when it was formed in 1947, serving overseas. As one member of the Yale class of 1941 put it, "Jim sort of went into the woodwork thirty years ago and hadn't been seen since -- until he surfaced the other day (1974)."

According to <u>Newsweek</u> Angleton began two decades as head of the powerful and mysterious unit whose task is to ensure that foreign intelligence agents do not infiltrate the CIA. He set up the CIA counterintelligence staff in 1954. By the late 1950s he had put together a large counterintelligence section divided into security, operations, research and analysis, liaison and such special sections as a Communist Party unit. During the 1950s the staff concentrated on the Soviet Union and its intelligence bureau, the KGB. In 1956 Angleton was responsible for obtaining a copy of Nikita Krushchev's secret speech denouncing Stalin. In 1967 he was put in charge of Operation Chaos, a program established by President Johnson to discover whether there was any foreign financing or manipulation behind the antiwar movement or any of the radical groups associated with it. Radical groups were infiltrated, computer files on subjects and individuals were established and extensive liaison with a similar office in the FBI was set up.

In the early 1970s, the CIA's executive director, William E. Colby, became concerned over Angleton's handling of counterintelligence and recommended his removal, stating that the super-secretive style of operation used by Angleton was no longer effective. This led to Angleton's resignation and retirement in December 1974.

The Newsweek article entitled "Angleton: The Quiet American" described him as follows:

> Angleton was an owlish man of 57 with a center part of hair, a neglected inch of ash on his cigarette and the slouch of a 6-footer gone prematurely to seed. Thick at the waist, sunken in the chest, he had an intimacy with modern poetry that, the new men were told, had included personal acquaintance with T.S. Eliot, E.E. Cummings and Ezra Pound [also born in Idaho]. He had an ironic face, wry and functional clothes that hung loosely on his stooped frame. In both build and looks he might have been the failed English professor of an Ivy League university. But the tight line to his thin mouth and his elliptic, sidelong habit of speech conveyed real experience. It was hard to place Angleton. ...He was not a man for all times, said an ex-agent. He was a man for one time. He was a man for the cold war.

Angleton died in 1987 but his ghost lives on in a book just published entitled Deception: the Invisible War Between the KGB and the CIA by Edward Jay Epstein.

BELL, Terrel H.   **1921-**   **Lava Hot Springs**

A farm boy from Idaho who rose to become a cabinet member under President Reagan, Terrel Howard Bell was born November 11, 1921 in Lava Hot Springs, a small town southeast of Pocatello, one of five sons and four daughters of Alta and William Bell. After graduating from Lava Hot Springs High School in 1940, Bell enrolled in the Southern Idaho College of Education, in Albion. His education was interrupted two years later when he joined the U.S. Marine Corps and was discharged in 1946 as a sergeant. Later that year he received his B.A. in secondary education. In 1954 Bell received his M.A. in educational administration from the University of Idaho and in 1961 his Ed.D. from the University of Utah.

Bell divided his professional career between the classroom and the administrator's office. He taught science and coached athletics at Eden High School in Idaho, 1946-47, and then became superintendent of the Rockland Valley (Idaho) school district, 1947-55. He moved to Afton, Wyoming as superintendent of the Star Valley school district.

In 1957 Bell became chief administrator of the Weber County school district in Ogden, Utah and in 1962 returned to teaching as professor and chairman of the department of education administration at Utah State University in Logan. From 1963-70 Bell served as Utah State Superintendent of Public Instruction.

In 1970 he joined the staff of the U.S. Office of Education and became acting commissioner the same year. President Nixon chose him to be the Commissioner of Education in 1974 and he was sworn into office on June 13, 1974 by HEW Secretary Caspar Weinberger. In 1976 Bell resigned this post to become Commissioner and CEO, Utah System of Higher Education. President Reagan named him Secretary of Education in 1981 and he served in that capacity until 1985.

He created the commission that wrote the 1983 report <u>A Nation At Risk</u> which warned of a rising tide of mediocrity in the schools and prodded many states to raise graduation standards and look for ways to improve teachers' status. Over twelve million copies of this report were disseminated.

Bell has written a number of books, the latest being <u>Thirteen Men, a Reagan Cabinet Memoir</u> published in 1988. A member of the UI Hall of Fame, Bell delivered the inaugural UI Founder's Day address in January 1988 and became the first recipient of the Founder's Day Award, given for service to higher education.

BEMIS, Polly   **1853-1933**   **Warrens**

The legend was that pretty little (about four feet tall) Polly was won in a poker game by Charley Bemis, a Warrens saloonkeeper and fiddler for square dances. But the fact was that Bemis, son of a prominent physician, won only her heart while she treated him for wounds suffered in a fight growing out of a poker game. Eleanor Wilson-Wagner writes of her in Central Idaho Magazine (Spring-Summer, 1988):

> Sometimes legends start small. This one was only broomstick high and beautiful. She had silky dark hair, almond eyes and skin the color of cream. She was a Chinese dance hall girl and her claim to fame began on a blustery night in Warrens, Idaho when she was the pot of a poker game. The game was between her Chinese master, Hong King, and Charley Bemis, a prominent saloon keeper.
>
> Her real name was Lalu . . . Lalu Nathoy, but in Warrens they called her Polly. The day she arrived in Warrens with two other Chinese women and her Chinese master, a big bearded stranger lifted her off her horse and christened her little Polly: a simple name for a nineteen year old girl who would someday be famous.
>
> She was born on a farm near the banks of a river in the Hong Kong region. Her family may have been well-to-do when she was a child, for her feet had been bound. At that time in China, crushed feet were considered sexually stimulating -- even beautiful.
>
> Then in 1867, when Lalu was fourteen and still innocent, her family fell on hard times. For several years there was drought in China and besides that, time and again soldiers pillaged the countryside, robbing the Nathoys of their crops and animals. Since one lame son was worth twenty beautiful daughters, her father had to sell her into bondage so the rest of the family could survive.
>
> Life was never innocent again for Polly. In Hong Kong she was sold to a company which shipped Chinese slave girls to Gold Mountain in America. She was smuggled into Portland, purchased by Hong King, and in 1872 he brought her and the other Chinese women to Warrens as an exotic attraction for his saloon.

After Polly nursed Bemis back to health they were married by the justice of the peace in Warrens, August 13, 1894, and left Warrens for a small and lonesome homestead on the Salmon River, at the mouth of Crooked Creek. There, in a deep canyon, they lived for years off the land. After Charlie's death in 1922 Polly continued to live alone in the little canyon cabin her husband had built. There she heard her first battery-powered radio, a gift from old friends at Warrens. In 1923 friends took her to Grangeville where she saw the wonders of a railroad, automobiles, and motion pictures. Then in 1924 came the trip to the big city of Boise where Polly stayed at the Idanha Hotel. She died November 3, 1933 at age 81 and was buried in Prairie View Cemetery in Grangeville. She was re-interred during the summer of 1986 at the homestead which has been made into a museum. Thousand Pieces of Gold, a book on her life by Ruthanne McCuun, may be made into a movie. The historic Polly Bemis house, which is only accessible by boat on the Salmon River, was recently nominated for inclusion on the National Register of Historic Places.

BENSON, Ezra Taft   **1899-**   **Whitney**

An Idaho farm boy who could drive a team of horses by the time he was five and later became Secretary of Agriculture in the Eisenhower Administration is now head of the 6.4 million member Church of Jesus Christ of the Latter-Day Saints.

Ezra Taft Benson was born August 4, 1899 on the family farm at Whitney, the son of George Taft and Sarah Benson. He is remotely related to the former U.S. Senator Robert A. Taft and is a descendant of Mormon pioneers. His grandfather was an advisor to Brigham Young during the Mormon migration to Utah in 1847.

Benson attended elementary school at Whitney and from 1914-1918 attended the Mormon Oneida Stake Academy in Preston. He studied at Utah State College in Logan, 1918-21, and went on a mission for the church to Great Britain. On his return he attended Brigham Young University and received a B.S. degree in 1926. He received his M.SC. in ag economics from Iowa State College (Ames) in 1927 and pursued graduate studies at the University of California.

In 1929 Benson became a county agricultural agent at Preston for the UI Extension Service and in 1929-30 was employed as extension economist and marketing specialist of the UI Extension Division. He was instrumental in organizing the Idaho Cooperative Council, of which he was secretary 1933-38. In Washington, D.C., where he represented this group, his work attracted national attention, and led to his appointment in 1939 as executive secretary of the National Council of Farmer Cooperatives, a post he retained until 1944.

He had been President of the Boise Stake of the LDS Church in the late 1930s and was similarly involved in Washington, D.C. where he headed the Washington Stake from 1940-43. Upon being selected in 1943 as a member of the Quorum of Twelve Apostles, the ruling body of the Mormon Church, Benson returned to Salt Lake City and disappeared from the national spotlight. On November 24, 1952 President-elect Eisenhower appointed him Secretary of Agriculture and he served until 1960.

He remains active in the LDS and was named President in 1985. Office: Church of Jesus Christ Latter-Day Saints. 50 N. Temple St., Salt Lake City, UT.

BLAKLEY, Ronee Sue   **1945-**   **Caldwell**

From Miss Caldwell in 1967 to Academy Award nominee for best film actress in 1975 -- that was accomplished by Ronee Sue Blakley of Caldwell. Her father, Ron, was from the Caldwell area and her mother, Carol, from Kansas. They met in Caldwell, were married in 1942 in Pendleton, and moved to Seattle where he got a job in a shipyard. They moved to Corvallis, where Ronee Sue was born in 1945, and back to Caldwell in 1954 where they have lived since.

Ronee attended Caldwell High School and in 1967 was selected Miss Caldwell. She attended Mills College on a scholarship her freshman year and then transferred to Stanford where she graduated with honors. Ronee also received a degree from the Juilliard School of Music.

She began playing piano at the age of eight. <u>The Illustrated Who's Who of the Cinema</u> states:

> Ronee Blakley is a tall, slim attractive brunette whose film performances seem as yet
> to be a sideline to her main career as a singer and composer. After studies at Stanford
> and Juilliard School of Music, she spent a year acting in Boston. In 1969 she gave
> a recital at Carnegie Hall. Blakley wrote her first film score, "Welcome Home,
> Soldier Boys," and issued her first album in 1972.

Ronee also began playing in clubs in the Los Angeles area in 1971. When she showed director Robert Altman some of the songs she had written for his film "Nashville," he asked her to appear in the film, in her first screen role.

She played the part of Barbara Jean, the neurotic country-western singer. For this role Ronee received the Academy Award nomination for best actress in 1975. "Nashville" has been called "Perhaps the most complex modern picture ever made." One of the songs she sang in this movie was "My Idaho Home."

Ronee was one of the stars of Bob Dylan's Rolling Thunder Tour in 1975. She has sung and acted in several other movies since then.

BOLLINGER, Elizabeth Anne   1919-62   Lewiston

World famous lyric soprano and Metropolitan Opera star Anne Bollinger was born December 22, 1919 in Lewiston. She was the daughter of William Bollinger who built the Bollinger Hotel there, which he operated until his death in 1924. She was known as Betty to her friends, but used the name Anne Bollinger professionally.

After graduating from Lewiston High School in 1937 she attended Ward-Belmont School at Nashville, Tennessee for one year. She attended UI for two years and two summers (1938-40) before transferring to the University of Southern California to complete her B.A. in music. While at UI she was a member of Sigma Alpha Iota, national music honorary, and a member of Kappa Kappa Gamma sorority. She sang in the Vandaleers and participated in other music activities.

Her professional singing debut was at the Hollywood Bowl in 1944 and the following season she appeared again under the direction of Leopold Stokowski. A runner-up in the finals of the Metropolitan Opera Company auditions she was awarded a $500 scholarship and a six-month's option with the Met and signed a contract in 1948. Earlier she had sung at Carnegie Hall and made her operatic debut in the role of the Countess in Mozart's "Marriage of Figaro" with the Pittsburg Opera Company. She had sung with the New York City Opera Company.

Her Metropolitan Opera debut was in "Carmen" on January 1, 1949. Anne Bollinger sang with the Met for four years and after her second season she spent summers singing in Central America. She left the Met for further study and recitals in Europe. In 1955 Anne Bollinger opened the Hamburg Opera house in Germany, a courtesy never before extended a foreigner. While singing there for three years she also gave performances in Switzerland, France, Austria, Italy, England and Ireland.

On February 1, 1956 she married Shell Oil executive Jack Nielsen and they made their home in Zurich. They had two sons. Although she continued her operatic career with frequent concert and television appearances in Europe, Anne was a regular visitor to the US and Lewiston. She "launched" the 1949-50 Moscow Community Concert series September 29, 1949 at UI's Memorial Gym and was, according to The Argonaut, the only alum to have achieved success with the Metropolitan Opera.

In Beacon for Mountain and Plain, Rafe Gibbs wrote:

Prior to her coming to the University, she wrote Registrar D. D. DuSault:

"I started out majoring in chemistry, but I didn't precipitate well in that subject. I think my future lies in voice."

How right she was! Anne Bollinger sang with the Vandaleers adding luster to that brilliant singing organization. In 1948, the pert, vivacious blond soprano, reached the American top -- the "Met." Later, in 1955, she would be the star who opened the glittering new opera house in Hamburg, Germany. But meanwhile, in 1949, she came back to sing at the University of Idaho. The <u>Lewiston Tribune</u> reported:

"Her music had not arrived in time for a program to be printed so she announced her own numbers. She gave the title of her first selection and added, 'Can you hear me?'"

"As the beautiful young Lewiston girl stood there, a voice boomed through the crowd: 'Baby, we don't have to hear you as long as we can see you!'

"She said it was the happiest recital she had ever sung."

There was standing room only at the Lewis Clark Normal School auditorium at her last two concerts in Lewiston on January 28 and February 11, 1962. She was fighting cancer and these proved to be the last concerts of her career. One of her encores at the last concert was the "Hills of Home" and she told the audience "You know which hills I mean." She never lost her love for Lewiston and the West. Anne Bollinger succumbed to cancer July 11, 1962 in Zurich, age 42.

BORAH, William E.   **1865-1940**   **Boise**

Probably the most widely-known politician to come out of Idaho was Senator William E. Borah, the "Lion of Idaho." Born June 29, 1865 in Fairfield, Jasper Township, Illinois, one of ten children, the Boise lawyer became Dean of the U.S. Senate, a member of the body for thirty-three years and served as Chairman of the Senate Foreign Relations Committee from 1921-40. Following elementary school at Tom's Prairie, Borah attended Southern Illinois Academy and the University of Kansas (1885-87). Current Biography (1940) says:

> While a student at the University of Kansas he "cut grass, waited on tables, and did odd jobs" to finance his way through law school. In 1890, as an accredited member of the Bar, he went to Lyons, Kansas and started to practice law. Day after day his office remained empty, and he gave the citizens one year to become clients. After that he closed up and, impelled by the inherited urge to "go West," decided to seek his fortune in Seattle. A chance acquaintance on the train suggested that he stop at the thriving Western metropolis of Boise, Idaho (pop. 2,500). There Borah saw a drunken lawyer trying a case and decided that if a drunken lawyer could succeed, a sober lawyer ought to make a living.

Borah's first love was the theater and his first ambition was to be an actor. As a young boy he once ran away from home and joined a Shakespearean company in which he played Mark Anthony. When he arrived in Boise, with $15.75 in his pocket, it "was a raw frontier town, and its horse stealing, cattle rustling, vice, gambling and gunplay gave the young lawyer plenty of practice." His prior Shakespearean training helped make him an outstanding orator and debater. His prosecution of "Big Bill" Haywood and others on charges of killing Governor Steunenberg in 1905 brought him national fame. The defense counsel was Clarence Darrow of Chicago.

In January, 1907 Borah was elected to the U.S. Senate, by the Idaho Legislature, where he served until his death in 1940. Borah had served as secretary to Governor McConnell of Moscow and married McConnell's daughter Mary in 1895. They had no children. Borah never used coffee, tea or tobacco and totally abstained from liquor. Borah seldom went out socially and never entertained. He lived so simply he was thought to be a poor man. So there was much surprise at announcements that he had amassed $207,000 in life insurance and government bonds at his death. "Borah of Idaho" died January 19, 1940 and is buried in Boise.

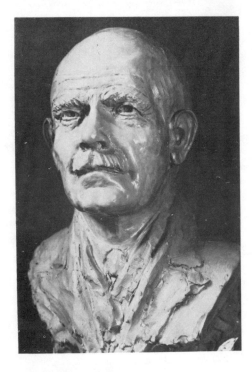

BORGLUM, Gutzon   **1867-1941**   **Bear Lake**

The world's largest sculpture was done by a man born in Idaho. The sculpture is one of America's most cherished monuments -- Mount Rushmore in the Black Hills of South Dakota. Here, on the summit of a 6,200 foot mountain, the gigantic carved heads of America's four greatest presidents, Washington, Jefferson, Lincoln, and Theodore Roosevelt, stand silent and proud as a "Shrine of Democracy." Each of the four granite figures is about 100 feet high and each noble countenance is 60 feet from the top of the head to the tip of the chin, twice as large as the ancient Great Sphinx of Egypt. The entire titanic sculptured panel measures 300 feet by 500 feet with the faces carved to the proportion of men 465 feet tall. Lincoln's mouth is 22 feet wide and a person can stand erect in Jefferson's eye.

The sculptor was John Gutzon de la Borglum, born March 25, 1867 at Ovid, near Bear Lake. After studying art in San Francisco, he worked in Paris, London and New York. Borglum was a well-known sculptor with more than 150 works to his credit as well as experience in executing mountain sculptures when he undertook his magnum opus. This work of the world's largest sculpture, which involved the removal of over 400,000 tons of granite and cost a little less than $1,000,000, took 14 years (1927-1941) to complete.

Borglum's parents left Denmark for America in 1864 and after a brief stay in New York City they headed west and built a cabin at a frontier settlement near Bear Lake. The family moved to Ogden when Gutzon was a child, and later to Nebraska, where he attended public schools in Omaha and Fremont, and St. Mary's College in Kansas. Later he was a student under Rodin in France. He returned to New York City in 1901 and built a studio there and his fame began to spread. Other major works included the Sheridan Equestrian in Washington, D.C. and the colossal marble head of Lincoln in the U.S. Capitol rotunda. The Mt. Rushmore monument has been called "the grandest sculptural project conceived and executed by man." Borglum, for whom Mt. Rushmore was the consummation of a life-time work devoted to his art, died, before it was completed, at Stamford, CT, March 6, 1941, age 74. When Borglum died, his son Lincoln (also a sculptor), was left with the responsibility of spending the final congressional appropriation on the project. Because of World War II some of the final touches, such as Washington's coat, were never completed. Lincoln Borglum had worked seven years on the project with his father, starting as a pointer. He later worked up to foreman and then superintendent. When construction stopped in 1941, Lincoln became the Memorial's first National Park Service Superintendent until 1944. Lincoln died in January, 1986, age 73.

BOYINGTON, Gregory (Pappy)   **1912-88**   **Coeur d'Alene**
                                                        St. Maries

The top Marine Corps flying ace was born and raised in northern Idaho. His career in World War II was
followed in <u>Time</u>, <u>Life</u>, and <u>Newsweek</u> from about 1944-47. <u>Time</u> (Jan. 10, 1944) reported:
> A bent-winged, big nosed Corsair fighter slid down the South Pacific Sky to the Bougainville
> runway. A balding disgruntled pilot hopped-out. Marine Major Gregory Boyington had just shot
> down his 25th Jap plane over Rabaul. But he had expected better hunting; he was still
> one short of tying, two short of beating, the U.S. record of 26 enemy planes shot down, a
> record held jointly by WWII Captain Joe Foss and WWI Captain Eddie Rickenbacker. "Pappy"
> Boyington stomped off the jungle-hemmed field, vowing that he and his Corsair would buzz
> up every day until they notched a new mark.

The next issue of <u>Time</u> reported the 30-year old Boyington went down over Rabaul, New Britain:
> The Corsair flashed down in the sunlight above Rabaul, with guns blazing. Its target,
> a Zero, burst into flames and plummeted toward the blue. That was the 26th victory for
> Maj. Gregory Boyington, leader of the Marines' Black Sheep Squadron. But pilots who
> saw the Zero fall lost sight of Boyington's plane. And a search that day and all the
> next -- in which the Black Sheep Squadron participated -- failed to find him. Including
> six planes he shot down as a Flying Tiger in China, the missing flier's tally of
> 26 kills equalled the American record for this war previously set by a fellow Marine,
> Maj. Joseph J. Foss, and also that for the last war established by Capt. Eddie
> Rickenbacker. Born at Coeur d'Alene, Idaho (Dec. 4, 1912), the 30-year old flier
> known as Pappy went down only a few days before his age would have probably forced
> him out of combat.

Nothing more was heard until the war ended and he was rescued after 20 months in a Japanese prison
camp, returning home a hero and to a four page spread in <u>Life</u> (Oct. 1, 1945). He was later credited with
two more downed planes, and awarded the Congressional Medal of Honor and Navy Cross. Boyington
was determined to be a flyer since his first flight at the age of eight with a barnstorming pilot at St.
Maries, where he lived for a time. He graduated from Lincoln High in Tacoma and the University of
Washington (1934) with a degree in aeronautical engineering. He worked a year as a draftsman at
Boeing, then took his Marine training, and in 1941 joined the Flying Tigers in China. He rejoined his old
Marine outfit in 1941 when the US entered the war and was commander of the famous Black Sheep
Marine Squadron which later was the basis for the TV movie "Flying Misfits" and the 26-episode TV series
"Black Sheep Squadron." Boyington later lectured and toured to promote his books, <u>Baa Baa Black
Sheep</u> (1957) and <u>Tonya</u> (1960), about his experiences with the Flying Tigers. He became a brewing
executive in Los Angeles and later a vice president for an aerospace manufacturing company until
retiring in the 1960s. He died in Fresno, CA, Jan. 11, 1988, and is buried in Arlington National Cemetery,
just down the hill from the Tomb of the Unknown Soldier.

BRINK, Carol (Ryrie)   **1895-1981**   **Moscow**

One of Idaho's best known fiction writers and certainly Moscow's most notable, Carol Ryrie Brink was born and raised in Moscow, attended UI from 1914-17, and wrote some thirty novels, many with an Idaho setting. Caddie Woodlawn, published in 1936, won her the coveted Newberry Medal for the year's most distinguished contribution to children's literature. She was awarded an honorary Doctor of Literature degree from UI in 1965. Brink Hall and the children's room in the Moscow/Latah County Library system are named after her.

Carol Brink was born December 28, 1895, the daughter of Scottish-born Alexander Ryrie and Henrietta Watkins. Ryrie had come from Scotland at the age of twenty and went west to settle in Idaho before it became a state. There he married Henrietta, daughter of a pioneer doctor, and became the first mayor of Moscow. Both of Carol's parents died before she was eight and she was raised by her grandmother and an unmarried aunt at 124 N. Polk. Alex Ryrie died of consumption in 1900. A year later, Dr. Watkins was murdered and in 1904 Henrietta, in despair over a hasty and unfortunate second marriage, committed suicide. Carol had a lonely but not unhappy childhood. It was Grandma Watkins who passed on the stories of her childhood in pioneer Wisconsin that gave Carol the love and appreciation of storytelling. Carol spent much of her time reading and making up her own stories. While attending the UI she wrote for the Argonaut as the society page editor. Finding Moscow too small she finished her college education at the University of California, Berkeley where she received a B.A. in 1918. That same year she married UI math professor Raymond Brink who later taught math at the University of Minnesota and was well known in his own right for the numerous math texts that he wrote. The couple made their home in St. Paul, Minnesota for many years. (On a personal note the author lived just five blocks from their home at 2243 Hoyt, but as a child was unaware of their reputations). In retirement the Brinks moved to LaJolla, California in the 1960s and she died there August 15, 1981.

Between 1936 and 1977 Carol Brink wrote nearly 30 books for children and adults, mostly fiction. Seven of them -- three children's and four adult's -- deal with accounts of life in and around Moscow. All Over Town, Louly, and Two Are Better Than One are happy children's books of her days in the town. Her trilogy of adult fiction based on Moscow history is darker, containing as it does the accounts of her family's tragedies. Buffalo Coat deals with the murder of her grandfather. The second Idaho novel, Strangers in the Forest, published in 1959, and Brink's last book, Four Girls on a Homestead -- a work of non-fiction published in 1977 -- are based upon the experiences of Carol's aunt on her timber homestead near Clarkia. Strangers gained popular national acclaim and was condensed by Readers Digest.

The last of the Idaho trilogy, Snow in the River, appeared in 1964, and Brink recounts the events surrounding her mother's suicide. The book examines Moscow during its later history, when both the town and the University had matured considerably since the period of Buffalo Coat.

BROOKS, Mary T(homas)   **1907-**   **Gooding/Boise**

This future Director of the U.S. Mint was born in Colby, Kansas in 1907 and came to Idaho with her family in 1909, arriving on New Year's day. Her father, who would later become a U.S. Senator, organized the First National Bank of Gooding and later became Mayor of Gooding.

Mary Thomas attended Mills College and graduated from the UI in 1929 with a B.A. She married Arthur J. Peavey, Jr. in 1930 who died in a hunting accident in 1941. Her son, Idaho State Senator John Thomas Peavey, manages the family sheep and cattle ranch. She also has a daughter, Betty Anne (Mrs. Gordon Eccles) of Picabo. In 1945, she married Wayland Brooks, U.S. Senator from Illinois. For a time she served as business manager at Mills College. She was a member of the Republican National Committee from 1956-63 and served as chairwoman in 1965. Elected as the only woman to the Idaho State Senate, she served District 21 from 1964-69 at which time she was named Director of the U.S. Mint, a position she held until 1977. She was named Idaho Woman of the Year in 1969 and inducted into the UI Hall of Fame in 1970. Mary T. Brooks resigned as Director of the U.S. Mint in February, 1977 to return to Hailey where she operated a sheep and cattle ranch. Just prior to her resignation, in January 1977, she received the Alexander Hamilton award, the highest award the Secretary of the Treasury can bestow, "in recognition of superior and unusual leadership" in the work of the department. She was the first woman to receive this award. During her tenure as Director of the U.S. Mint, the production of coins almost doubled from seven billion units in 1969 to over thirteen billion coins in 1975. Various denominations of bills in the 1970s carried her signature. She is a member of numerous civic, social and political organizations, was appointed by Gov. Evans in 1985 to the Idaho Resources Board, and in August 1988 received the American Numismatic Association's highest honor, the Award of Merit. She now resides in Boise.

Her father, John R. Thomas, was appointed on June 30, 1928 by Governor H.C. Baldridge to succeed the late Senator Frank R. Gooding and he won a six year term in the election later that year. On January 27, 1940 he was appointed by Governor C.A. Bottlfsen to succeed the late Senator Borah and was re-elected to a six year term in 1942. He was considered an "old line" Republican and resisted the expansion of governmental activities brought about by President Roosevelt's administration. In many ways his political thinking matched that of his predecessor, Borah, though he was less of an orator and less forceful. He was engaged in the livestock and banking business and died of a cerebral hemorrhage, at age 71, in Washington, D.C. on November 10, 1945.

BROOKS, Phyllis   **1914-**   **Boise**

Boise-born Phyllis Brooks was a leading lady in the movies during the 1930s and 1940s starring with Joel McCrea, Chester Morris, Randolph Scott, Ethel Merman, Shirley Temple and others. Her most famous role was in Rebecca of Sunnybrook Farm in 1938.

Her father was an industrial engineer, her mother a drama coach, and she was born Phyllis Weiler, July 18, 1914. She became a model to pay for her tuition in a Chicago art school, after having attended schools in St. Paul, Milwaukee and Grand Rapids.

She was brought to the screen in 1934 by Universal Studios to play opposite Chester Morris in I've Been Around. According to the book They Had Faces Then, about superstars and starlets of the 1930s, she "had the kind of petulant blonde-good looks you expected to see in a magazine." And, "There's not much to say about her acting except that she was an adequate actress when called upon to act. . . but she was decorative in pictures." In 1936 she played the part of Jean Maitland (Ginger Rogers in the movie) in Stage Door on Broadway. She also appeared in Broadway plays like Panama Hattie in 1940 with Ethel Merman, The Night Before Christmas in 1940 and Round Trip in 1945.

Rebecca of Sunnybrook Farm was a black and white 20th Century Fox picture in which Phyllis played the part of Lola Lee. It was basically a vehicle for Shirley Temple and the original story was changed to display her talents. Shirley was ten at the time and her singing voice never better. Among the songs she sang were "On the Good Ship Lollipop," "When I'm With You," and "Animal Crackers."

Phyllis' other pictures included:

McFadden's Flat (1935)   Shanghai Gesture (1941)
You Can't Have Everything (1937)   Hi Ya Sailor (1943)
Charlie Chan in Reno (1939)   The Unseen (1945) with Joel Mcrea
Slightly Honourable (1940)   High Powered (1945)

In 1945 she married Harvard football star Torbert MacDonald and retired.

BURROUGHS, Edgar Rice   1875-1950   Pocatello

The internationally known author of the <u>Tarzan</u> series and other types of popular fiction, including crime stories and westerns, once ran a stationery and cigar store and delivered newspapers on horseback in Pocatello.

Edgar Rice Burroughs was born September 1, 1875 in Chicago and later attended Michigan Military Academy. In 1889 his brothers Harry and George bought a ranch in Cassia County, along the Raft River, 30 miles from American Falls, from Yale classmate Lewis Sweetzer. Edgar joined them in the mid-1890s and experienced the frontier west firsthand, doing everything from mending fences to driving cattle.

Through brother George he received a principal appointment to West Point but failed the medical exam in June 1895. As things were heating up between the U.S. and Spain he determined to get into the military and spent some time in the U.S. Army cavalry but returned to Idaho in 1898.

In June of that year, with the moral support and capital provided by brother Harry, Edgar purchased a stationery and cigar store from long time Pocatello resident Victor Roeder, at 233 W. Center St. It had a newsstand and cigar-counter, and specialized in the sale and rental of Kodak cameras, photographic materials, books, magazines and newspapers. He even established a delivery service for newspapers and delivered them himself, on a black horse named Crow, when he could not find someone else to do it. Despite his enthusiasm, the business did poorly and in early 1899 he sold it back to Roeder saying "God never intended me for a retail merchant."

Once again unemployed, he turned to creative writing and the rest is history. Before leaving Idaho he spent another year on the Mule Shoe Ranch on the Snake River with his brothers. Then he worked briefly for a dredging company in Minidoka in the Stanley Basin in 1903, and in Parma (1904) where he ran for office in a Canyon County election and lost.

Having married Emma in Chicago in 1900, and now with a family to feed, he moved to the Southwest and eventually to California and spent the rest of his life writing, undoubtedly influenced by the way of life and his experience in Idaho. His adventure writings sold more than 100 million copies in fifty-six languages. <u>Tarzan of the Apes</u>, for which he is best known, first appeared serially in 1912 and in hardcover form in 1914, and was his second novel. By the end of his career in 1944, Burroughs had published about seventy novels. He died March 19, 1950.

CANNON, J.D.   **1922-**   **Salmon**

Described in one of the biographical directories of the theater as the "Cold-eyed American character actor," J.D. Cannon of Salmon has appeared in dozens of stage plays, films, and TV programs over the past four decades. He is probably best remembered as the cigar-smoking chief of detectives on "McCloud."

John Donovan Cannon was born April 24, 1922 in Salmon, the son of a miner. He graduated from Salmon High School in 1940 and studied acting at the American Academy of Dramatic Arts from 1940-42 and the American Theater Wing, 1949-50. He served in the U.S. Army from 1942-45 and held the rank of tech sergeant.

<u>Notable Names in the American Theater</u> (1976) has a lengthy biography of Cannon and lists his theater, film and television performances. Before going into the theater, Cannon worked as a ranch hand, sheepherder, guide and restaurant cashier. He appeared in over thirty stage plays from 1955 to 1966. The plays were mostly Shakespeare, mostly in New York and Phoenix.

In 1966 he began to appear in motion picture films, including:

An American Dream, 1966   Cool Hand Luke, 1967
Heaven With a Gun, 1969   Krakatoa, East of Java, 1969
1,000 Planes Raid, 1969   Cotton Comes to Harlem, 1970
Lawman, 1971   Scorpio, 1973
Raise the Titanic, 1980   Death Wish II, 1982

Cannon appeared as Detective Chief Peter B. Clifford, Sam McCloud's (Dennis Weaver) cigar-smoking boss, from 1970-76 in the television series "McCloud." He also appeared in a number of other series including:

The Defenders   The Nurses
The Untouchables   Wagon Train
Naked City

Cannon's office is in Beverly Hills.

CATALDO, Fr. Joseph M. (S.J.) 1837-1928   Lewiston, North Idaho

Called the "Last of the Black Robes," Fr. Cataldo became Jesuit Superior of the Rocky Mountain Missions, and served as peacemaker in the Nez Perce War (1877).

Born in Sicily, March 17, 1837, he contracted tuberculosis and, at age two, funeral arrangements were made. But he lived. Cataldo had a consuming desire to become a priest and, against the wishes of his father, he entered a Jesuit seminary at age 15. He was a sickly child and a consumptive all his life. While studying to be a Jesuit he fell ill and was given the last rites and ordained on his death bed. Again, he lived. He remained to finish his studies until 1862 and then volunteered for missionary work.

In 1863 he was sent to the U.S. -- California. From there Fr. Cataldo was sent in 1865 to the Rocky Mountain Mission to live among the Coeur d'Alene Indians. He was then sent in 1866 to Lewiston where he built the first church for whites (St. Stanislaus) in northern Idaho and the Mission of St. Joseph at Culdesac, for the Nez Perce.

Proficient in the Nez Perce language, he gave his sermons twice, once in English and again in Nez Perce. He wrote one of the first books in Nez Perce and served as peacemaker in the Nez Perce war meeting with Chief Joseph and General Howard.

He became Superior of the Rocky Mountain Mission in 1877 and made his headquarters at the Old Mission of the Sacred Heart, located at Cataldo a few miles east of Coeur d'Alene, just off today's I-90. This church was later named after Fr. Cataldo. Its construction began in 1847 and is the oldest existing building in Idaho. It is now a state park.

Fr. Cataldo founded Gonzaga University in 1881, paying $2.60 an acre for the land, and is considered one of the founders of Spokane. Some local residents still recall Fr. Cataldo saying Mass at churches in Moscow, Genesee and Lewiston in the 1920s. A week long celebraton was held in Spokane in his honor in 1928 for his 75th anniversary as a priest. He appeared at Gonzaga, on the stage at the Pantages Theater and there was a dinner for him at the Davenport Hotel.

The man who was not expected to live through his childhood died April 9, 1928 at Pendelton, Oregon, age 92. He is buried at Mt. St. Michael's in Spokane.

CHURCH, Frank   1924-84   Boise

After Senator Borah, Frank Forester Church was probably Idaho's most notable politician; he was grandson and namesake of a pioneer who settled in the Boise area during the gold-rush days following the Civil War. Church was born July 25, 1924 in Boise to Frank Forester Church II and Laura Bilderbach. Laura's father was a sporting goods store owner and a conservative Republican who generally denounced the liberal domestic policies of then President Franklin Delano Roosevelt. To make life interesting and stimulate family debate young Frank would take the other side of political issues and after doing some research on issues at the public library became a New Deal supporter, even though Senator Borah always remained his political hero.

As a high school junior, Church won a first prize college scholarship in the American Legion's 1941 national oratory contest and afterward toured Idaho to demonstrate his public speaking talent. He entered Stanford University in 1942 but in his first year there left to join the U.S. Army as a private in WWII. Following officer training at Ft. Benning, GA he was commissioned a second lieutenant in the infantry and later was assigned as a military intelligence officer in Asia. After the war he returned to Stanford where he won honors in debate, was elected Phi Beta Kappa and received his BA, in 1947. That same year he entered Harvard Law School and after the winter returned to Stanford for the milder climate. In 1948 he was diagnosed as having cancer and given six months to live. X-ray treatments and surgery restored his health and he received his LL.B. from Stanford and in 1950 gained admittance to the Idaho bar. He entered the firm of Langroise, Clark and Sullivan, and practiced law for the next six years in Boise, while teaching public speaking at Boise Junior College. He lost a bid for a seat in the legislature in 1952 and while still relatively unknown entered the race for the U.S. Senate defeating former Democratic Senator Glen Taylor in the primary and incumbent Senator Herman Welker in the election of 1956 to become the youngest member of the Senate, at age 35. Church was chosen the National Jaycee Outstanding Young Man in 1957 and gave an inspiring keynote address at the 1960 Democratic Convention which brought him into the national spotlight. He went on to serve with distinction in the Senate, serving on many important committees, and was Chairman of the Senate Foreign Relations Committee from 1979-1981. The UI awarded Church an honorary LL.D. in 1967. In 1976 he ran for the Democratic party presidential nomination but lost. He was unseated by Steve Symms in the 1980 senatorial election and died of cancer April 7, 1984 at Bethesda, MD.

During his thirty-four years in the Senate Church was one of the first prominent critics of US intervention in Southeast Asia, and sponsored much legislation concerning water needs of Idaho, conservation, and social welfare, particularly the problems of the aging. He headed a Senate probe that revealed extensive violations of individual liberties by the CIA, FBI, and other intelligence agencies.

COBB, Tyrus Raymond   **1886-1961**   **Twin Falls**

Major league baseball player Ty Cobb amassed more individual records than any other man. "The Georgia Peach" was born December 18, 1886, the son of a state senator and grandson of a Confederate army officer, on his grandfather's farm near Narrows, GA. He was reared and educated in Royston where his father became superintendent of schools.

Cobb's boyhood dream was to become a surgeon and his earliest athletic interest was track. He was playing schoolboy baseball at 12, later joining the teenage Royston Rompers.

In 1904, at age 18, he was offered a tryout with the Augusta Club. In 1905 Cobb led the South Atlantic League in stolen bases (40) and batted .326. Then Detroit bought Cobb for $700 and he played for the Tigers twenty-two years (1905-26) and was playing manager 1921-26.

He led the American League in batting twelve years, had a lifetime batting average of .367 and stole 892 bases. He was the first player elected to the Baseball Hall of Fame at Cooperstown, NY in 1936. His last two playing years were with Connie Mack's Philadelphia Athletics.

When he retired in 1928 he had participated in 3,033 games, more than any other player. He became one of the highest paid players of his era. His annual salary rose from $1,500 in 1906 to $70,000 and, having invested wisely, he retired a millionaire. He is one of three called the greatest baseball player of all time: some say Babe Ruth, some say Ty Cobb and others Honus Wagner.

Cobb was always helpful in advising younger players. At the September 1947 Old Timers Game in Yankee Stadium, he demonstrated he could still lay down a bunt, at age 61.

He lived in various places after retiring from baseball. Cobb is listed in the 1949 Twin Falls telephone directory (247 Shoup) and old timers remember that he owned the Coca Cola Bottling and Distributing Co. there, which was run in the late 1940s by his second son Herschel, who served as vice president.

Ty Cobb died July 17, 1961.

DAVIS, A(rtemus) D(arius)   **1905-**   **Burley**

Albertson's, Safeway, and Wynn-Dixie are large, national grocery chains started by individuals with Idaho connections.

The Wynn-Dixie chain in 1987 was the seventh largest chain with 1275 stores in the US and about $8 billion in annual sales, and the principal food distributor in the Southeast U.S.

It was started by A. D. Davis who was born in Burley, November 22, 1905. Davis began his career in the grocery business in 1917 as a delivery boy. He and his three brothers and his father started in business for themselves in Miami, Florida in 1925.

In 1939 they purchased control of the Wynn & Lovett Grocery Co, of Jacksonville and built it into one of the largest grocery chains in the nation. By 1967 the four Davis brothers, all of whom graduated from UI in business (J.E. '28, A.D. '29, Austin '34, and Tine '38) had built their 720 store network in the Southeastern part of the U.S. into the billion dollar club with annual sales of $1,020,000,000.

For many years the Davis brothers provided scholarships for students in business administration at UI and in 1980 Davis established the A. Darius Davis Free Enterprise Award made annually to a UI faculty member through the College of Business and Economics. The award recognizes work that contributes to the preservation and improvement of the free enterprise system. The cash award amounts to about $20,000 annually. Two-thirds of this amount is paid in recognition of recent work and one-third is made available for summer research support.

Davis received an Honorary LLD from UI in 1961 and he was a member of the executive committee and chairman of the National Association of Food Chains. In retirement Davis owned and operated a cattle ranch in Florida. He lives in Jacksonville.

DISNEY, Lillian Marie Bounds   190?-   Lapwai/Lewiston

In his biography of Walt Disney, Leonard Mosley explains that the Disney brothers (Walt and Roy) were considered confirmed bachelors when they pooled their $300 savings with a $500 loan from their uncle Robert Disney and converted a small garage into a studio. Walt Disney (1901-66) was born in Chicago and grew up on a farm in Missouri where he learned to love animals. At age twenty he was working as a cartoonist for the Kansas City Film Ad Company. Soon afterwards he formed his own company, Laugh-O-Grams, there in 1922. His business manager-brother had tuberculosis and went to convalesce in Arizona and then Los Angeles. Walt moved (July, 1923) to California and lived for a while with his retired uncle Robert Disney in Edendale. He had some stationery printed "Walt Disney, Cartoonist." In 1924 "Disney Productions" had another cartoonist and "three girls that do inking."

Walt and Roy were very frugal and shared a one-bedroom apartment. Walt didn't like Roy's cooking and told him so continually. One night Walt ended up with a plate of stew on his head with Roy saying "I'm finished! No more cooking. No more of your goddamned complaints." The next day Roy wired his long-time fiance in Kansas City: WHAT ARE WE WAITING FOR STOP WHY DON'T YOU COME OUT HERE AND TIE THE KNOT STOP. Roy and Edna Francis were married at the home of Uncle Robert, April 11, 1925, four days after her arrival. Walt was best man and Lilly Bounds, an inker at Disney Productions, was the maid of honor, at Walt's request. Now living by himself, Walt Disney "was the most undomesticated of young men -- he did not cook, could not make a bed, and was completely unaware that dust and dirt accumulated in an unattended household." He began dating Lilly Bounds. One night she complained about his old Ford car and Walt said "Lilly, would you rather have me buy a new car for both of us or an engagement ring for you?" Lilly replied without hesitation, "An engagement ring."

Lilly was born in Lapwai and attended elementary school there. She went from Lewiston to LA to visit a married sister in Edendale and liked California. A neighbor of her sister suggested Lilly try to get a job at Disney Productions. She was hired as an inker at the prevailing wage of $15 a week and quickly learned the painstaking routine of "inking and painting" the celluloid, a tedious and eye-aching job since sixteen frames of celluloid had to be inked and painted for every single movement of a cartoon character.

Lilly and Walt were married July 13, 1925 at the home of her brother, who was the fire chief, at Lewiston. She is credited with naming the famous screen character Mickey Mouse. Walt had picked Mortimer Mouse.

Lilly has made many contributions to civic and community projects in Lapwai and the Lewiston area. She and her two daughters manage Retlaw (Walter spelled backwards) Enterprises, Inc., which owns KLEW-TV in Lewiston, KIDK-TV in Idaho Falls, and four other CBS affiliated television stations in Fresno, Monterey, Yakima and the Tri-Cities.

DUBOIS, Fred T.   **1851-1930**   **Blackfoot**

Idaho Territorial Delegate, and later Senator, Fred Dubois played a major role in Idaho politics for over three decades and in gaining Statehood. Rafe Gibbs' Beckoning the Bold explains statehood:

On a warm summer day in 1890, in Washington, D.C. (before air conditioning), U.S. Senators eased into congressional committee seats to listen to an address. They figured the speech would at least be tolerable, because it would be given by Fred T. Dubois, Idaho Territorial Delegate, who had done well as a student orator at Yale and had been improving ever since. Dubois declared:

"These people of Idaho, who have subdued the desert and the forest, who have wrenched untold millions from the solemn and reluctant hills, thus aiding struggling humanity everywhere, who have borne the hardships which have opened up an empire for thousands of homes, are the worthy descendants of their fathers of the revolution, and seek now by petition what these fathers gained one hundred years ago by arms and blood, the right of self-government..."

Before he finished, Dubois was perspiring freely. When the showdown came on the afternoon of July 1, 1890, the act adding a forty-third star to the American flag for Idaho breezed through the Senate (it passed earlier in the House) by voice vote.

Dubois carried the bill himself to President Benjamin Harrison for signing on July 3 but asked him to hold it for a day because "Our people almost unanimously wish to become a state on the Fourth of July." After Harrison explained the star of a new state goes on the flag on the Fourth of July following the date of admission to the Union, Dubois changed his mind and had the President sign on July 3, 1890 saying "I want the star of Idaho on the flag tomorrow."

Dubois, son of a prominent Illinois attorney general, graduated from Yale and went to Idaho in 1880, settling in Blackfoot. He served as a U.S. Marshall from 1882-86 and was elected to Congress as a Republican in 1886. In 1888 he persuaded Congress to reject a proposal to divide Idaho between Nevada and Washington. He was elected U.S. Senator in 1890 and became a national leader of the Silver Republican party. During the Spanish-American War he was an anti-imperialist. In 1900 he allied with and took over the leadership of the Idaho Democratic party, though still officially a Republican. He then became a Democrat but supported President Theodore Roosevelt on progressive domestic issues, such as conservation. He was defeated in 1906 over anti-Mormon issues but retained national prominence and managed Champ Clark's national campaign for the Democratic presidential nomination in 1912, and was President Wilson's manager for the western states in 1916.

PHOTO: L-R. Fred Dubois, Wm. Jennings Bryan, Ira B. Perrine.

EARP, Wyatt   **1848-1929**   **Murraysville/Eagle**

Gambler, horse thief, saloon keeper, and sometimes lawman, Wyatt Earp spent time in the Coeur d'Alene Mining District in 1884 wheeling and dealing in Idaho real estate.

Wyatt Benny Earp, who won fame as a gunfighter in the American West, was born March 13, 1848 in Illinois. After the Civil War he worked as a teamster, buffalo hunter, and policeman in Missouri and Kansas. In 1880 he arrived in Tombstone, Arizona with his brothers Virgil and Morgan and his friend Doc Holliday. There they became involved with the Clanton family in the famous gunfight at the OK Corral where Wyatt killed three men on October 26, 1881. The Earp brothers and Holliday were all technically deputy marshalls, whose guns were hired to bring peace to Tombstone. A friendly Justice of the Peace ruled that the marshalls had killed the cowboys in the line of duty but a lot of folks thought otherwise. So it was time for the Earps and Doc Holliday to get out of town. Holliday settled in Leadville, Colorado where he died of tuberculosis at age thirty-six, in 1887. The Earps drifted to Idaho, landing in the Coeur d'Alenes tent city of Eagle.

Wyatt brought his six shooters and handlebar mustache with him to Idaho and got into a shooting fracas over a real estate deal in Eagle. His lead-throwing ability wasn't what it had been in Tombstone, and earlier in Dodge City. He didn't even ruffle his opponent, William Buzzard of Spokane. In Eagle, Wyatt and his brother James ran a saloon called the White Elephant. Housed in a white tent as big as a dozen elephants, the saloon did a rip-roaring business. Nobody got out of hand. Wyatt Earp may not have been able to hit Buzzard with one shot, but nobody wanted to test him on a second. The Earp brothers poured what money they made from the White Elephant, some from fast shuffling of cards, into mining ventures and town properties. Shoshone County legal documents signed by Wyatt Earp during the period February 1-December 26, 1884 deal with mining claims, land and property during the 1883-84 gold rush there. Records in Wallace disclose that he was a locator of the following lode mining claims in the Murraysville and Eagle City area:

      Consolidated Grizzly Bear - May 10, 1884   Dead Scratch - May 18, 1884
      Dividend - May 11, 1884   Golden Gate -June 1, 1884

The brothers never made much on these and in fact, Wyatt, who died broke January 13, 1929 in California, age 80, still owes Idaho a tax bill.

An ad for the White Elephant appeared in the July 18, 1884 issue of the <u>Weekly Eagle</u> of Eagle City as follows:

      Largest and finest appointed saloon in the Coeur d'Alenes. Earp Bros., Proprietors (with) finest brand of foreign and domestic liquors to be found in the U.S. Call and see the Elephant.

EDMUNDSON, Clarence   **1882-1964**   **Moscow**

Clarence (Hec) Edmundson was more than another local boy who "made good." He was also a UI student who gained local admiration and national recognition as an athlete and coach.

Edmundson began his UI athletic career in 1901 when he enrolled in the prep school. He was a member of the track team for five years -- three as a prep school student and two as a college student. Conference rules ended his participation before graduation. While at the UI, Edmundson set school records in the 440 yd., 880 yd., and mile runs and was AAU champion in the half-mile event. He was continually used in the quarter-, half-, mile, and relay events. A 1908 Argonaut story stated that Hec had lost only two races in his career to that point; one was run after he had been ill with blood poisoning and the other loss occurred when he was required to run two long races within a quarter of an hour. After his graduation Edmundson became a teacher and basketball coach at Broadway High School in Seattle. He maintained his status as a distance runner during this time and, sponsored by the Seattle Athletic Club, participated in the 1908 Olympic Games in London and the 1912 Olympic Games in Stockholm, reaching the finals in his events. He had become America's premier 1/2 miler.

In 1913, UI proudly acquired her favorite athletic son as an instructor in practical agriculture and track coach. That the "doer" could also be a teacher became evident when Idaho's track record improved in a short time. By 1916, Edmundson was also the basketball coach, and a successful one. In a sense, Hec Edmundson was responsible for the athletic nickname of Idaho's teams. In 1918, sports editor McCarty of the Argonaut referred to Edmundson's basketball team as "Heckmen," then "Heckers." Following a surprise victory over a strong Gonzaga team, he changed the named to "Wreckers." Dean Hulme was reminded of an earlier group of wreckers -- the Vandals -- and Idaho teams acquired a name.

Hec Edmundson left Moscow in 1919 to assume coaching duties at Texas A & M and then the University of Washington. His subsequent career with the Huskies was illustrious, resulting in ten Northern Division track trophies and ten Northern Division and three Pacific Coast Conference basketball championships in twenty-three years. In 1934, the Helm Athletic Foundation named Edmundson as one of the ten all time great basketball coaches. Edmundson Pavillion at the University of Washington is named after him.

Edmundson's name was associated with UI once more, in 1955. A charter member of the Idaho chapter of Kappa Sigma fraternity, he was honored guest and speaker at Kappa Sigma's fiftieth anniversary celebration. At that time, the fraternity established an annual athletic trophy and award to be known as the Hec Edmundson Inspirational Football Player Award. Hec Edmundson was on hand as President Theophilus accepted the award for UI during the half-time ceremonies of the 1955 Idaho-WSU game. Edmundson is credited with starting the racehorse style of basketball and creating the five man handshake. He died August 6, 1964 in Seattle.

ELSENSOHN, Sr. M. Alfreda, OSB   1897-1989   Grangeville

Since she won her first prize of $10 for a history of the Pomeroy School District in 1914, Sr. Alfreda had been writing and teaching all her life until her retirement. Born February 7, 1897 in Grangeville, Edith M. Elsensohn, was the daughter of Lewis and Mary (Bosse) Elsensohn. Her father was a pioneer school teacher in Peola, Keuterville and Cottonwood and the first superintendent of public schools in Idaho County. Although she had written a number of books she was best known for her two volume Pioneer Days in Idaho County published by Caxton in 1947 and 1951.

She moved from Grangeville to Pomeroy with her family at age eight and entered the order of St. Benedict at St. Gertrude's Convent, Cottonwood, in 1915 when she was eighteen. Most of Sr. Alfreda's life was spent teaching, writing and in study. She graduated from Lewiston State Normal School in 1924, attended Washington State College and graduated with a B.S. in education from Gonzaga in 1929. She taught at Cottonwood, Ferdinand, Keuterville, and Colton Catholic Schools and for over twenty-five years at St. Gertrude's Academy and Junior College. She also served as vice president of the junior college in the 1950s and established the historical museum there in 1931 and directed it for many years. Sr. Alfreda received an M.S. from UI in 1939 with a major in botany. In connection with that work she published Flora of Idaho County which was used as a textbook in science. With the help of her science classes she started the outstanding museum at St. Gertrude's with many mounted specimens. The museum contains some famous collections, such as the Polly Bemis collection, large stamp collections, and precious stones and metals from all over the world.

While taking a geology and geography class at UI, she included in a report articles of historical information and her instructor encouraged her to incorporate pioneer history of the county into a series. This led her to write Idaho County Place Names which was submitted to Caxton Printers in 1943. The Caldwell firm suggested changing the name to Pioneer Days in Idaho County. From an early age, Sr. Alfreda was entranced with Idaho County's heroes and lawbreakers and her father encouraged her to write a history of the county, which is the largest in Idaho and larger than many states. She interviewed many old-timers, studied old newspapers, diaries, letters, store accounts and other resources. In her book the past lingers on in the famous old mining towns of Florence, Warren, Dixie, Elk City and Orogrande.

Sr. Alfreda had given numerous lectures all over the state and received many awards including the Silver Jubilee award of the Catholic Library Association in 1958, the Inland Empire Press-Radio-Television award in 1959, the Idaho Territorial Commission award in 1969 (also named Idaho Writer of the Year), the Governor's Award in 1970 and named "Distinguished Citizen" that same year. She was a member of numerous professional organizations and listed in Who's Who Among Northwest Writers, Catholic Authors, Personalities of the West and Midwest and numerous other biographical directories. Sr. Alfreda retired at St. Gertrudes in Cottonwood, where she died April 12, 1989 at the age of 92.

ENGLEHORN, Shirley   1940-   Caldwell

Caldwell's lady golfer won nearly $200,000 during her professional career from 1959-80. After winning four successive tournaments in 1970 <u>Sports Illustrated</u> had a two page spread on her and told how she became a golfer:

> Shirley grew up in Caldwell, Idaho, which is not exactly a sunshine-the-year-round golfing capitol. Her family lived beside the third-hole of the municipal course, and Shirley started to play the hole when she was seven. "I would sit on a bank and watch until the hole was empty, then run out and play it," she remembers. Before too long she was going around the whole course, and by the time she graduated from high school, she was ready to join the tour, which she did soon thereafter.

As an amateur Shirley won the Idaho Open four times, the state championship in 1956 and 1957 (age 16-17) and the Pacific Northwest championship in 1959. Her professional career lasted from 1959-80 which is amazing considering the number of injuries she had during this time. In 1960 she fell off a horse and fractured six vertebrae. She could not swing comfortably for a long time but did win her first tournament in 1962.

In 1965 she was in a serious automobile accident and had compound fractures of her heel and ankle. Six months passed before she could rejoin the tour, and when she did her ankle still bothered her. In 1967 and 1968 she underwent surgery to remove screws from the damaged bones. In 1967 she won the Ben Hogan award given for her achievement in returning to winning golf (just as Hogan did himself after a serious accident). From 1962 to 1970 she was only once not in the money list top ten, her most effective years being 1969 when she was fourth; and 1970 when she was third and also won the LPGA (Ladies Professional Golf Association) tournament. Thereafter the 29 year old Caldwell golfer entered tournaments spasmodically as she turned to teaching golf. She was named LPGA Teacher of the Year in 1978.

The <u>Sports Illustrated</u> article entitled "Fine till the nerves go 'Ding'," said four wins in a row were enough to show that Shirley Englehorn - gimpy ankle, wobbly putter and all can rival the best on the ladies' tour. The article explained about tournament pressures:

> The pressure set in two nights before the tournament. Shirley was in her motel room, watching a Joan Crawford rerun and massaging her sore left shoulder with what she thought was Absorbine. Suddenly she leaped from the bed. Her left shoulder and left arm were black. "I realized," she said "that I was using shoe polish to massage my arm. Ding-a-ling."
> Then she began dropping things. Everything she picked up she dropped. In the morning she scattered golf balls all over the club parking lot. On the course she left a trail of pencils, tees, score cards, gloves and ball markers. "And I'll bet that I've had to change my dinner clothes at least once a night because I've spilled something on them," she said. "At least she's wearing her success well," another player noted.

FARLEY, Carole   **1946-**   **Moscow**

Moscow-born soprano Carole Farley has become one of the most sought after singers of her generation, a super-star in the major opera houses of Europe. According to a 1972 publicity release "Carole Farley has just become the youngest leading soprano in the history of the Cologne Opera. She will appear in the title role of 'Lulu,' a most flattering assignment for an American." Farley set a record at the Cologne Opera of fifteen curtain calls on opening night for her performance. Ten years later she sang the lead in the acclaimed Paris production of the "Merry Widow" over fifty times -- the first time an American sang the lead role in France. She is a principal singer at the Metropolitan Opera where she made her debut in 1977 in the demanding role of "Lulu" -- a role she has repeated more than eighty times in three languages, German, English and French, including the first European production in Zurich. She has also starred in film versions of operas.

Farley regularly appears in the world's foremost opera houses including the Chicago Lyric, New York City Opera, Canadian Opera and the opera houses of Cologne, Zurich, Dusseldorf, Paris, Turin, Buenos Aires, Nice and Florence. Her many roles include Massent's "Manon," Mozart's "Idomeneo," Verdi's "La Traviata," Offenbach's "Tales of Hoffman." She has made orchestral appearances with most of the leading orchestras in the U.S. such as the New York Philharmonic, Boston Symphony, Philadelphia Orchestra, Cleveland Orchestra, Pittsburgh Symphony, Minnesota Orchestra, Baltimore Symphony, and many more. Farley's eight recordings include "Beethoven's 9th Symphony" under Antal Dorati, with the Royal Philharmonic, and "Vienna Dances" with Andre Kostelanetz for CBS records.

Born in LeMars, Iowa, November 29, 1946, Carole moved with her family to Moscow in 1953 and began studying with her mother, Irene, who taught in the public schools for twenty-two years. She graduated from Moscow High School in 1964. The slim, blonde, strikingly attractive and vivacious soprano soon gave evidence of her wide-ranging talent by winning the State Junior Miss Contest. She sang in the UI Summer Chorus and did office work in the UI Agricultural Economics Department. Her father Mel is a professor emeritus of Education at UI. After earning a B.S. in music from the University of Indiana in 1968, Carole received a Fullbright Scholarship to study music in Munich (1968/69), and began singing professionally in 1969.

Her parents moved from Moscow to Coeur d'Alene in 1980 and have travelled to many countries to see and hear her perform. Farley presently lives in New York and London with her husband, conductor Jose Serebrier.

FARNSWORTH, Philo T.   **1906-71**   **Rigby**

In September, 1983 the U.S. Post Office issued a block of four 20 cent stamps honoring American inventors -- Charles Steinmetz, for his electrical theories, Edwin Armstrong for frequency modulation, Nikola Tesla for the induction motor and Philo T. Farnsworth for the first television camera. Farnsworth is the only Idaho personage depicted on a postage stamp besides Chief Joseph and Ernest Hemingway.

Born August 19, 1906 in Beaver, Utah, Farnsworth was educated in the Utah and Idaho public schools and while at Rigby High School in 1921, delved into the molecular theory of matter, electrons, the Einstein theory, and studied automobile engines and chemistry. In 1922 he came up with a practical system of television broadcasting (the cathode - ray tube or dissector tube) for which he later received basic patents and recognition as an inventor of television. He finished high school in Provo and in 1924 entered Brigham Young University but left at the end of his second year due to the death of his father.

Farnsworth was inducted into the National Inventors Hall of Fame in 1984 (there is only one other member with an Idaho connection, Lew Sarett, q.v.) and the write up says of him:
> In 1926 he joined the Crocker Research Laboratories in San Francisco to take all the moving parts out of television. At the age of 20 he produced the first all-electronic television image. Crocker Research Laboratories was later reorganized as Television Laboratories, Inc., and in May 1929 was renamed Farnsworth Television, Inc., of California.
> His basic television patents included scanning, focusing, synchronizing, contrast, controls and power. The first patent #1,773,980 entitled Television System, was filed January 7, 1927, and was granted August 25, 1930. He also invented the first cold cathode ray tubes, and the first simple electronic microscope. He used radio waves to get direction (later called radar) and black light for seeing at night (used in World War II). During the 1960's he worked on special purpose TV missiles, and the peaceful uses of atomic energy. Before his death, he worked on a nuclear fusion process to produce clean, virtually unlimited, energy on which he held two fusion energy patents. When he died at age 64, he held over 300 U.S. and foreign patents which made possible today's TV industry, the TV shots from the moon, and satellite pictures.

In 1939 agreements were signed with Philco and RCA and his invention enabled NBC to transmit America's first television program from the New York World Fair.

There is a museum in Rigby dedicated to him and his work and signs outside Rigby proclaim it the "Birthplace of Television." Philo T. Fransworth died March 11, 1971 in Salt Lake City and is buried in Provo. His widow, Elma, and son, Kent, who attended UI in the early 1950s, published a book about Farnsworth in 1989 entitled Distant Vision.

FERY, John Bruce　　　　　　　**1930-**　　　　　　　**Boise**

Boise Cascade, the multi-billion-dollar forest products company based in Boise, was founded by Robert Hansberger in 1957. (Originally incorporated as Boise Payette Lumber Co. in Delaware -- Apr. 23, 1931. Present name adopted May, 1957). When Fery took over the helm of the company in 1972 it was in financial trouble. Boise Cascade lost $170.6 million that year and the losses included a $210 million write-off of recreation community property in California. As president and CEO he had to pull in the reins on the company's wide-ranging businesses and concentrate on building materials and paper products. When, in 1977, John B. Fery was named one of the ten best chief executive officers of U.S.- based corporations by Financial World, it was strong acknowledgement by the business community that Boise Cascade Corp. had come full circle. Fery doesn't think diversification is bad and did not fault the decision of previous management to diversify operations into Latin America and into real estate development. He just felt his company would be better off working towards opportunities for growth in the paper and wood products businesses.

John Fery was born February 16, 1930 in Bellingham, Washington. After serving in the U.S. Navy in 1950-51 he received his B.A. from the University of Washington in 1953, his MBA from Stanford in 1955 and an LLD from Gonzaga in 1982. He began his career in business in 1955 as Assistant to the President of Western Kraft Corporation and joined Boise Cascade in 1957. Having served as President from 1972-78, Fery was then chosen Chairman of the Board and CEO. He was named most outstanding CEO by Financial World in 1977, 1978, 1979, and 1980. Fery serves on numerous boards of directors and advisory councils including Albertsons, Hewlett-Packard, the Moore Financial Group, the American Forestry Institute, the Stanford School of Business, and St. Alphonsus Hospital. He received the honorary Doctor of Natural Resources degree from UI in 1983.

Asked why Boise Cascade Corporation continues to maintain corporate headquarters in Boise rather than, New York City, which is closer to the money market, an AP story quoted Fery as saying it's easier to commute home, sometimes even from New York:

> John Fery, board chairman and chief executive officer of the multi-billion-dollar (Boise Cascade Corp.), recently attended a business meeting in New York; arrived in Boise by company Lear jet for a 2:30 p.m. appointment; drove home to watch his son, Michael, play a junior high football game, and then dropped back into the office for some catch-up work. "You couldn't do that if the company's corporate headquarters were in New York," Fery said. "It would be just too much of a hassle to get out to the suburbs for a junior high school football game. And once you got home it wouldn't be practical to go back to the office for a little while."

His office at Boise Cascade Corporation is at 1 Jefferson Square in Boise.

FISHER, Vardis   **1895-1968**   **Annis, Hagerman**

One of Idaho's most prolific (nearly forty novels), best known and truly distinguished writers, Vardis Fisher was born March 31, 1895 in Annis and lived in Hagerman. His novels, set in the Rocky Mountains, were praised for their psychological realism and historical accuracy. Fisher's best known works include Children of God (1939) on the history of Mormonism, and The Mothers (1943) about the Donner Party. Fisher also wrote a twelve-volume series of novel's on mankind's spiritual and intellectual history, called the Testament of Man (1943-60).

"Old Irascible" wrote his own biography for Twentieth Century Authors (1942) which is quoted here in part:

> I was born on a wild windy night that ushered in All Fool's Day a few minutes later;
> in a one-room cottonwood shack on a bleak Mormon outpost in Idaho; with a caul which
> for my mother augured that I'd be a bishop at least and perhaps an apostle. Nursed
> on a cow, allowed to yell night and day, and despised by relatives for whom I was
> the most sickly runt in a pioneer clan, I headed straight into the most introverted
> childhood that ever had nightmares on an American frontier. To the age of ten or
> eleven, when I first entered school, my memories are chiefly of howling wolves,
> screaming cougars, venison, deer skins for bedding, and neighborless loneliness.
> My father, Joseph, and mother, Temperance Thornton, stemmed from Mormon converts who
> went with Joseph Smith. I have one brother, Dr. V. E. Fisher, a psychologist, and
> an atheist like myself; and a sister, Irene, who is pious enough for a whole tribe.
>
> I took a B.A. from the University of Utah; an M.A. and Ph.D. (magna cum laude) from the
> University of Chicago. I have taught in those and in other universities. My doctoral
> thesis was on the literary reputation of George Meredith. No linguist, I had a deuce
> of a time learning Old English and German. I was corporal in the first war to save
> democracy but never got shot at.
>
> My career began, I suppose, early in high school; for before I was half way through a
> wild-eyed and sentimental adolescence, I wrote what I called a novel, as well as a ton
> of horrible verse. Inasmuch as by that time I had an incurable feeling of infer-
> iority, I decided to be a writer. I read so much before the age of thirty that I nearly
> went blind, and that great and noble scholar, John Matthews Manly, pointed out to me

that I was a book drunkard. Doubtless many authors have influenced me for good and
ill. I think of Keats, Meredith, France, Cabell. My only literary preference is
for intelligent books.

And that goes for persons. I belong to no political party, no societies or clubs. My
political convictions are summarized in the last chapters of <u>No Villain Need Be</u>.
My favorite public figures are men of integrity like George Norris. My chief
dislikes include evasions in their multitude of forms; increasing taxes that
assume the dubious privilege of being governed to be worth all the tribute it costs;
college graduates who, unable to find a job, set up as literary critics;
dictatorships and any suppression anywhere of freedom of thought and voice; the
sentimental chivalry of a nation that encourages parasitic women; radio advertising; and
my own books as soon as they are finished. I like intelligence; persons who
do not think with their emotions; and persons who discipline their egoistic demands with
a rebuking sense of irony.

The thrice married Fisher in 1935 directed the Federal Writer's Project in Idaho and almost single-handed
wrote the <u>Idaho Guide</u> and the <u>Idaho Encyclopedia</u>. After 1940 he and his third wife, Opel Laurel
Holmes, lived in the Thousand Springs Valley where, without assistance, they built their own home and
several other structures.

Fisher was a close friend of Thomas Wolfe and was often compared to him. He died July 9, 1968 in
Hagerman.

FOOTE, Mary Hallock   **1847-1938**   **Boise**

The nationally-known Western novelist, essayist and illustrator, Mary Hallock Foote had already established a reputation when she came to Boise in 1884. Born November 19, 1847 in Milton, New York, of Quaker parents, Mary Hallock was raised on the family farm in the Hudson River Valley. After completing her schooling in 1864 she enrolled at New York City's Cooper Union to study art. Over the course of three years there she prepared herself for a career in black-and-white illustration. Her first professional drawings appeared in 1867 in A. D. Richardson's <u>Beyond the Mississippi</u>. In the next twenty-five years she executed drawings for some of the most prominent books of the period including titles by Longfellow, Hawthorne and Whittier. By the 1890s she was considered the "dean of women illustrators" and was elected to the National Academy of Women Painters and Sculptors. In 1867 she married Arthur De Wint Foote (1849-1934) who became a successful mining engineer. She followed him to California, Colorado and Idaho, where they lived in and around Boise from 1884-95.

She gained professional recognition in the early 1870s as an illustrator in national magazines. By the end of the century she was nationally recognized as a leading writer and illustrator of the American West. While in Idaho she wrote two novels - <u>The Chosen Valley</u> (1892), about the building of a dam in the Snake River Valley and <u>Coeur d'Alene</u> (1894), based on the struggle between the miners and mine owners of North Idaho. Her life in Idaho provided background for novels and frontier situations. Many of her stories were first published in <u>Century</u> magazine. Income from one novel enabled the Footes to build their "Stone House in the Canyon" in 1885. This house was the site of an archaeological excavation in the summer of 1986 by the UI Anthropology Laboratory and a museum exhibit of the house travelled throughout Idaho in 1987 and 1988.

Arthur Foote was born into a prominent Connecticut family and became a successful mining engineer at a young age. After working in California and Colorado, he designed an irrigation project that brought the family to the Boise Canyon. The project involved the construction of seventy-five miles of irrigation canals which would irrigate 350,000 acres of farmland between the Boise and the Snake rivers. However, he was unable to secure the financing and finally gave up in 1895 and moved to Grass Valley, California where he continued his former career as a mining engineer. His irrigation canal was eventually completed in 1909 and still irrigates the Boise Valley.

Even after she and her husband moved to California, Foote continued to write about Idaho, e.g.:
      <u>The Cup of Trembling</u> (1895) - two volumes of adult stories about the lives of early
      Idaho cowboys, ditch riders, miners, trappers, and daughters of ranchers.

The Little Fig-Tree Stories (1899) - Idaho fiction for children.
The Desert and Other Sown (1902).
A Touch of Sun and Other Stories (1903).
Edith Bonham (1917) - a fictionalized autobiography based on her Boise years.

After The Ground-Swell (1919) she ceased writing novels. During the 1920s, when she was nearing eighty, she wrote her memoirs which were published posthumously in 1972 by the Huntington Library under the title A Victorian Gentlewoman in the Far West. This helped reawaken interest in Foote as did Angle of Repose, a Pulitzer Prize winning novel by Wallace Stegner, based in part on her life, published in 1971.

In 1988, Idaho State University Press published The Idaho Stories and Far West Illustrations of Mary Hallock Foote. The volume includes ten stories and their settings include Boise, Glenn's Ferry, the Arco desert, Coeur d'Alene mining district and the Pocatello area.

Foote died June 25, 1938 in Hingham, Mass.

FRENCH, Burton L.　　　　**1875-1954**　　　　**Moscow**

When the University of Idaho Board of Regents fired President Franklin B. Gault in 1898, one of the students at the time made the decision to enter politics and change the way regents were appointed. He did get things changed and went on to serve in the U.S. House of Representatives from 1903-33.

Burton L. French was born August 1, 1875 in Delphi, Indiana but his family moved when he was seven to Palouse, Washington. He entered UI in 1893 but did not graduate until 1901. At this time, the Regents were appointed for two-year terms at the same time by the governor. This meant a whole new board would come in with a new governor. Governor Frank Steunenberg, who became Idaho's most famous governor through death by assassination at the hands of Harry Orchard in a period of labor strife, selected a new board upon his election in 1897. The new Regents knew little of Gault (he was very popular at the time) and his work, and what they did know they did not like. After his dismissal, Gault became President of the University of South Dakota. In 1953 Gault Hall at UI was named for him. The decision to dismiss Gault was very unpopular among the UI faculty and students, and one student who took it very hard was Burton French.

French ran for and was elected to the Idaho House of Representatives in 1898. He introduced a bill abolishing the two-year appointment system, and providing for three regents to be appointed for six years, three for four years and three for two years. French was re-elected to the Legislature in 1900 and served as Republican floor leader during his last two years. After graduating from UI in 1901, he became a fellow in political science at the University of Chicago and earned an M.A. in philosophy. Returning to Moscow he ran for Congress and was elected in 1902 and served 1903-09, 1911-15, and 1917-33. French was finally defeated by Democrat Compton I. White in the landslide of 1932 and again returned to Moscow. In 1935 he accepted a teaching position in the political science department at Miami University in Oxford, Ohio. French continued teaching, and became department head, until his retirement there in 1946. At that time, President Truman appointed him to serve on the Loyalty Review Board. French received an honorary doctorate of Law from UI in 1922. He returned many times to the UI campus and on October 12, 1932 gave the principal address on the occasion of the UI's 40th anniversary. At this time he instigated an alumni campaign to restore on campus the old stone steps of the first Administration Building which was destroyed by fire in 1906.

French died of leukemia in Oxford, Ohio in 1954 at the age of 79 and is buried in Moscow. His diaries and other papers are deposited in the UI Library's Special Collections.

GALLOWAY, Dr. Thomas C. Jr.   1886-1977   Weiser

A young man from Weiser made his way by cattle car to Chicago and became a renowned surgeon. Thomas Galloway was born March 17, 1886 in Boise, the youngest of nine children, and grew up on the family farm near Weiser. He had a rugged childhood and adolescence in the old west, working hard on the family ranch. This may well have been a contributing factor to his sturdy physique and long life of good health. Galloway graduated from the University of Idaho with a B.S. degree in 1907 and taught chemistry the following year. He subsequently made his way by cattle car to the University of Chicago whose Rush Medical College was at that time attracting students from all over the United States. After acquiring a Master of Science Degree at the university, he went on to obtain his M.D., graduating from Rush in 1912.

An internship at Cook County Hospital was followed by three and one-half years in the U.S. Public Health Service. These experiences, plus two additional years as a Captain in the Army in World War I, provided a broad medical background which Dr. Galloway always regarded as having been influential in his subsequent career. Following the war, he served a residency in otolaryngology at Cook County Hospital, took post-graduate work in Vienna, and thereafter became an assistant to Dr. Robert Sonnenschein, one of Chicago's leading otolaryngologists. In his capacity he received the munificent salary of one hundred dollars per month.

Dr. Galloway moved to Evanston in 1921, and began what eventually proved to be a truly brilliant career. He became associated with Children's Memorial and Cook County Hospitals where he headed the staff in otolaryngology and taught for many years. He joined the staff of Evanston Hospital and continued to practice there for over fifty years. He had a distinguished career at Northwestern University Medical School and eventually became the director there. Galloway was the first to demonstrate conclusively the value of tracheotomy in the treatment of bulbar poliomyelitis. Widespread use of his methods is credited with the saving of hundreds of lives.

He was the author of numerous publications and the recipient of many awards including an Honorary Doctor of Science degree from UI in 1957, the Distinguished Alumnus Award from Rush Medical College and the American Laryngological Associations Newcomb Award.

In 1976, just after his ninetieth birthday he spoke at the American Laryngological Association and "charmed everyone and outshone all the younger men with his scintillating account of medical reminiscences."

At his ranch in Idaho, Dr. Galloway hosted family reunions each summer for fifty years. He died February 24, 1977, age 91, in Evanston, Illinois.

GHORMLEY, Robert Lee   **1883-1958**   **Moscow**

A Moscow man became the first Naval Commander in the South Pacific in World War II. In its Centennial edition, the <u>Daily Idahonian</u>, ran a story about Robert Ghormley, July 4, 1987, under the heading "Moscow's Most Famous Sailor Became an Admiral." It said in part:

> It was a bright fall day in October 1942. Moscow held a celebration for its own war hero -- Robert Lee Ghormley. "Buy a Bond for Bob" ran the fundraising slogan, and the town's residents responded, purchasing over $125,000 worth of war bonds in one day.
>
> "Moscow has done a splendid job," noted an administrator in charge of Idaho bond sales. "It is far more than would be expected from a town of this size."
>
> Moscow hosted a gala parade that day to honor Ghormley -- 1,500 marchers, led by three bands. Ghormley's brother and sister came from the West Coast for the festivities. After the parade, the crowd moved to Recreation Park near the University of Idaho campus.
>
> There Jay Glover Eldridge, one of Ghormley's professors at the turn of the century, served as master of ceremonies, dedicating the site as Ghormley Park.
>
> Robert Ghormley was not in Moscow that festive day. He was commanding all Allied naval forces in the Southwest Pacific, and at the time of the celebration was involved in intense fighting in the Solomons.

Ghormley was born October 15, 1883 in Portland and moved to Moscow in the mid-1890s when his father, Rev D.O. Ghormley, became minister of the Presbyterian Church. After graduating from Moscow High School, he attended UI where he was a charter member of Phi Delta Theta, the school's first fraternity; won Phi Beta Kappa honors, and lettered in football. Ghormley was a major in the student cadet corps, president of his 1903 graduating class, treasurer of the YMCA, and active in the UI Mandolin Club. He then entered the U.S. Naval Academy and graduated second in his class. After numerous naval assignments, Ghormley was named Commander of the U.S. fleet in the South Pacific. He retired in 1946 as a highly decorated Vice Admiral with two Distinguished Service medals and a Legion of Merit award, and returned to Moscow as commencement speaker that year at UI. Though he never lived in Moscow after leaving in 1903, Admiral Ghormley always considered it home and voted there by absentee ballot from wherever he was stationed around the world. He died June 21, 1958 and is buried in Arlington National Cemetery.

GILBERT, Alfred Carlton   1884-1961   Moscow

Moscow sent two young men to the 1908 Olympics. One was Clarence "Hec" Edmundson, q.v., and the other was A.C. Gilbert who won the pole vault, but later gained fame and fortune as the inventor of a toy called the Erector Set. In it's July 4, 1987 Centennial Edition, the Daily Idahonian article on Gilbert said:

> A. C. Gilbert moved to Moscow in the early 1890s when his father became president of the First National Bank of Moscow. Gilbert always loved athletics. In a barn behind his parents' house on Jackson street, he created a gymnasium complete with horizontal bar, tumbling mat, weights, wrestling ring, and punching bag.
>
> He practiced most on the punching bag and at the age of 12 ran away from home to join a traveling minstrel show where he was proclaimed "The Champion Boy Bag-Puncher of the World." A week later his father caught up with the show and brought A.C. back home.
>
> Not long afterwards, A.C. journeyed up the hill to the university where he saw his first pole vaulters in action. "I thought it was wonderful, soaring so high in the air just by using a pole," he later wrote. "They were probably jumping no higher than eight feet, but it seemed high to me, and I made up my mind to try it."
>
> One evening after dark, Gilbert walked out of town and stole a cedar rail from a fence. "I suppose the farmer who owned the fence was angry at finding part of it missing," Gilbert later reminisced, "but he made an important contribution to a later world's record and an Olympic championship without knowing it."
>
> About 1899, Gilbert left Moscow to attend preparatory school at Pacific University in Oregon. But he never relinquished his interest in pole vaulting. In 1904, he moved across the country to Yale to enter medical school, and there set world records in the pole vault in 1906, 1908, and 1909 (13' 2").
>
> Indeed, he revolutionized the sport. He was the first vaulter to replace hickory poles with springier bamboo. He was also among the first to vault without the use of a steel spike in the bottom of the pole. Instead, he dug a hole under the crossbar -- the forerunner of today's box -- and planted his pole prior to take off.
>
> In 1908, he became an Olympic champion at the games in London. He continued his interest in the pole vault long after those games, serving as manager of American Olympic teams in 1932 and 1936.

However, in 1912 A.C. Gilbert started a new career by inventing one of the most popular of all toys, the Erector Set. Over the years the Gilbert Toy Company marketed a variety of toys including chemistry sets, microscopes, American Flyer trains, and the Erector Sets and he became a millionaire many times over. The copy of his autobiography, The Man Who Lives in Paradise (Rinehart-1954), in the UI Library was received as a gift from Earl David of David's Department store. The book is inscribed to Earl David as follows: "With many happy memories of the days I spent with you in Moscow." Gilbert made his home in Hamden, CT and his office was at Erector Square, New Haven, CT. He died January 24, 1961.

GIPSON, Lawrence Henry   **1880-1971**   **Caldwell**

Idaho's first Rhodes Scholar once drove a stagecoach and later became an internationally known historian. Lawrence Henry Gipson was born December 7, 1880 in Greeley, Colorado and moved with his family to Caldwell where he spent most of his boyhood.

Gipson attended Caldwell High School and the Academy of the College of Idaho where he did long distance running. His father, Albert Gipson, edited the Idaho Odd Fellow and the Gem State Rural and Livestock Farmer. His brother, James Herrick Gipson, became President of Caxton Printers, Ltd. of Caldwell. A 1954 article on Gipson in Current Biography says:

> "While a youth in Idaho," he recalls, "I drove a stagecoach; I also learned the printing trade before entering the University of Idaho and to a great extent met my expenses by acting as a newspaper reporter." He won an oratorical prize, and a prize in English literature.
>
> Gipson received the A.B. degree in 1903 from the University of Idaho in Moscow. In the following year he successfully competed for the first Rhodes scholarship to be granted in Idaho. In 1907 he was awarded the B.A. degree from Oxford University in England.
>
> Upon returning to the United States, Gipson served as a professor of history for three years at the College of Idaho. He continued his studies at Yale University in New Haven, Connecticut as a Farnham fellow in history in 1910 and 1911. President James A. MacLean of the University of Idaho and President William Judson Boone of the College of Idaho, Gipson believes, were important influences in his choice of history as a field of endeavor.

At Wabash College, Gipson was a professor and head of the department of history and political science from 1911-24. He received his Ph.D. in history from Yale in 1918 and won the MacFarland prize for his dissertation which was published by Yale University Press in 1920 and was chosen for the Justin Winsor prize of the American History Society. Gipson became head of the department of history and government at Lehigh in 1924 and held that position until 1946. He was a research professor 1946-52, and author of a 15 volume history - The British Empire Before the American Revolution, written from 1936-70 for which he received the Columbia University Loubat prize in 1948, the Bancroft prize in 1950, and the Pulitzer prize in 1962. "Now that volume 8 is available ... the monumental character of Gipson's achievement is beyond dispute," from the NY Herald Tribune Book Review January 17, 1954. His 1954 address in Current Biography is 'The Library, Lehigh University, Bethlehem, PA." He wrote a number of other books and many articles for historical journals. He was awarded honorary doctorates from Temple in 1947, Lehigh in 1951, and the LL.D from UI in 1953. He died September 26, 1971.

GOFF, Abe   **1899-1984**   **Moscow**

One of Moscow's most distinguished political figures, Abe McGregor Goff, was born December 21, 1899 in Colfax, Washington. He played football for UI and graduated in 1924 with an LLB. A big part of his job as prosecuting attorney for Latah County from 1926-34 was to enforce the state prohibition laws. Goff served as a member of the Idaho State Senate from 1940-42 and was President of the Idaho Bar Association at the time he was called to active duty during World War II. He was a member of General Douglas MacArthur's staff during the occupation of Japan. While still in the service he was elected US Representative from Idaho and served one-term in Congress, from 1946-48. In 1958 President Dwight D. Eisenhower appointed him to serve on the Interstate Commerce Commission where he later became Chairman and served until 1967. Then he retired to Moscow - 503 East C St. Abe Goff was much sought after as a public speaker in Moscow. His papers and speeches are in the Special Collections Department, UI Library. Upon his death, age 85, November 23, 1984 the Idahonian eulogized:

> He cast a long shadow over life in the community in nearly 60 years of public service.
> He certainly had one of the most colorful and distinguished careers of anyone who has
> ever called Moscow home.

He enjoyed taking visitors through his den, a room added on to the side of his house, and showing them pictures of himself with US Presidents from Hoover to Nixon, and other dignitaries such as Emperor Hirohito, Haillie Selassie, etc.

His wife, Florence, was born December 27, 1908 in Honer, Minnesota and was distinguished in her own right. Her family moved to Moscow in 1908 and her father, George Richardson, was depot agent for the Spokane and Inland Electric Line and later became Mayor of Moscow. Florence attended Moscow schools and was a member of the last graduating class of the UI Preparatory School in 1913. She graduated from UI in 1917 and her class wrote the state song "Here we have Idaho." Florence wrote the words for the second verse. After graduation she became one of the first P.E. teachers in Moscow and later taught for three years at Boise High School. Florence returned to UI in 1924 to teach girl's gym and was director of the May Fetes. She and Abe married August 24, 1927 and she was an active participant in the Washington, D.C. social life while they lived there. She remained an active member of the Congressional Club until her death in Moscow, October 30, 1987.

HABIB, Philip Charles   **1920-**   **Moscow**

After being in the international spotlight for over six years as President Reagan's personal representative, Philip Habib returned in 1987 to private life. As presidential envoy, he worked toward peace in the Middle East, Philippines and Central America.

Prior to his position as envoy, he served as senior advisor to the Secretary of State (1979-81), Undersecretary of State for Political Affairs (1976-78), Assistant Secretary of State for East Asian and Pacific Affairs (1974-76), and Ambassador to the Republic of Korea (1971-74). Habib was considered to be the State Department's most knowledgeable expert on Southeast Asia.

The 1981 Current Biography article on Habib says:

> In May 1981 Philip C. Habib came out of retirement at the request of President Ronald Reagan to act as a special envoy in an attempt to extinguish the smoldering Lebanese civil war before it ignited a wider conflict between Syria and Israel. Habib, who played a major behind-the-scenes role in the formulation of American foreign policy during his three decades in the diplomatic corps, first came to public prominence in 1969, when he was named acting head of the United States delegation to the Paris peace talks that officially ended American involvement in the Vietnam war. An expert in Asian affairs, he turned his attention to the Middle East in 1977, after President Jimmy Carter asked him to help arrange the meetings between President Anwar Sadat and Prime Minister Menahem Begin that eventually resulted in the Camp David peace agreement ending hostilities between Egypt and Israel. At the time of his retirement in 1978, Habib was Undersecretary of State for Political Affairs, the highest position attainable by a career foreign service officer.

Born February 23, 1920 in New York City, of Lebanese descent, the son of a grocer, Habib grew up in the Bensonhurst section of Brooklyn and worked as a shipping clerk in a sheet metal factory before enrolling at UI where he received a degree in forestry in 1942. After that he enlisted in the U.S. Army. Habib had already begun a career in the foreign service as the third secretary at the U.S. Embassy in Canada (1949-51) when he completed his Ph.D. in 1952 from the University of California at Berkeley. He came out of retirement again in 1987 to serve as an honorary Co-Chairman of the UI Centennial Campaign. The former presidential envoy now lives in Belmont, California. He received an honorary degree from UI in 1974.

HARRIMAN, William Averell   1891-1986   Sun Valley

The man who founded Sun Valley was "born almost embarrassingly rich . . . and could easily have idled his life away as a dilettante without appreciably denting his family fortune. Yet Harriman . . . always heeded the command of his father, railroad magnate E. H. Harriman, to be something or somebody," from <u>Time</u> August 4, 1986.

<u>Current Biography</u>, 1946 says of him:

> To W. Averell Harriman's career of banker, railroad director, diplomat, and nonelective Government official, President Truman added in September 1946 the post of Secretary of Commerce, vacated shortly before by Henry A. Wallace. Under the Roosevelt Administration, Harriman had served as Lend-Lease coordinator between the United States and Britain, and as Ambassador to Russia; under President Truman, he had been Ambassador to Great Britain for a short period. Harriman, who had been born and bred a Republican, became a Democrat during Al Smith's campaign for the Presidency. He was also a close friend of President Roosevelt and was associated with the New Deal after its inception in 1932.
>
> The son of financier Edward Henry Harriman (who "feared neither God nor Morgan") and his philanthropic wife, Mary W. (Averell) Harriman, William Averell Harriman was born November 15, 1891. At seventeen, just when he was entering Yale from Groton, his father died, leaving him and his brother E. Roland Harriman various railroad holdings and a fortune reputed to be between seventy and one hundred million dollars. During summer vacations from college, the young millionaire worked as a clerk and a section hand in the Union Pacific Railroad yards at Omaha, Nebraska. Upon graduation from college in 1913, he once again went to work for the railroad, and in less than two years had risen to be vice president in charge of purchases and supplies for Union Pacific.
>
> Shortly before the United States entered World War I, Harriman bought a small shipyard at Chester, Pennsylvania, where he built the first partially prefabricated ships in the country. Out of this grew the Merchant Shipping Corporation, of which Harriman was chairman of the board. In 1920 the twenty-nine-year-old railroad and shipping magnate established W.A. Harriman and Company, a private bank. For the next decade Harriman was chairman of the board of this concern, but when it was merged with the Brown Brothers firm in 1931 to form Brown Brothers, Harriman and

Company, he accepted a partnership in the new corporation. (He had already disposed of his shipping interests in 1927 in order to devote more time to finance).

Harriman became chairman of the board of the Union Pacific Railway in 1932. During the depression of the thirties, while other railroads were retrenching, he poured millions into streamlined aluminum trains, low-priced diner meals, and trained-nurse stewardesses. As a result, at the lowest point of the depression, in 1934, Union Pacific's receipts from passenger traffic rose 66 percent. Two years later board chairman Harriman called in public relations man Steve Hannagan to look into the possibilities of establishing a winter resort on some thirty-three hundred acres of Idaho valley land owned by the railroad. The result was the famous playground Sun Valley.

Sun Valley was opened for business at Christmas in 1936. It was built like an Austrian ski resort, with Challenger Inn like an Austrian mountain village. Austrian ski instructors were brought in and the media was soon calling Sun Valley the St. Moritz of America. Famous people from all over the US began coming to Sun Valley for ski vacations, the world's first ski chair lifts were installed, and the Union Pacific ran special trains. Many movies were filmed at Sun Valley. It was described in a 1936 Collier's article as "The most elaborate of all Rocky Mountain resorts," and became a mecca -- summer and winter--for the famous, the wealthy and just plain ordinary tourists.

President John F. Kennedy once said that with the possible exception of John Quincy Adams, Harriman "held as many important jobs as any American in our history." He was an avid skier until his doctor ordered him to quit in his seventies. He never carried any cash and often left young Foreign Service officers "stuck with the tab" and thus gained the nickname from them as "the world's richest cheapskate." He died July 26, 1986, age 94, at Yorktown Heights, N.Y. His widow, Pamela Harriman, still maintains a summer home at Sun Valley.

HEMINGWAY, Ernest   **1899-1961**   **Ketchum**

Famed novelist, journalist and, writer of short stories Ernest Hemingway was born July 21, 1899 in Oak Park, Illinois. Upon graduation from high school there he chose journalism instead of college and spent seven educational months as a cub reporter for the Kansas City Star. Deficient eye-sight kept him out of the armed forces in WWI so he volunteered as a Red Cross ambulance driver in Italy which provided the theme and locale for one of his most successful novels, A Farewell to Arms (1929). He was severely wounded by shrapnel on July 8, 1918 and recuperated in Milan.

After the war he got a job with the Toronto-Star. He married Hadley Richardson in Chicago in September 1921 and in December they sailed for France and lived for nineteen months in the Latin Quarter of Paris, while he travelled extensively in Europe as a foreign correspondent for the Toronto Star. Late in 1923 they returned briefly to Toronto where their son John (Jack) was born.

Early in 1924 he resigned from the Star, returned to Paris and launched his career as a serious writer. He was the most conspicuous of the "lost generation," a group of expatriate American writers who lived in Paris in the 1920s. His first volume of short stories, In Our Time, appeared in 1925 and was followed by The Sun Also Rises (1926), Men Without Women (1927), A Farewell To Arms (1929) etc. He lived for 12 years in Key West, FL. after his divorce from Hadley in 1927.

Hemingway travelled in Europe and Africa before coming to Ketchum to live in 1960, although he had visited Sun Valley often since it opened in 1936. (For Whom The Bell Tolls was completed during one of his stays in Ketchum-Sun Valley). The Old Man and the Sea won him the 1953 Pulitzer Prize. Despite two airplane crashes that ended his second African safari (1953-54), his productivity continued into the late 1950s.

He left Cuba in 1960 for Ketchum where he and his fourth wife, Mary Welsh, had acquired a house. His mental and physical health had deteriorated by 1960 when he came to Idaho. The tragedy of Ernest Hemingay's last years was compounded by alcoholism and illness, including diabetes, (which in 1929 prompted the suicide of his father, a physician who knew there was no effective treatment of the disease in his day). Despite repeated hospitalizations, Hemingway failed to recover fully. He died of a self inflicted shotgun wound in his home, July 2, 1961. He is buried in the Ketchum cemetery.

The filming of a television mini-series of the final years of his life started in late August, 1987, in the Sun Valley-Ketchum area. The six-hour production of "Hemingway" was aired in late May, 1988 and starred Stacy Keach as Hemingway and Pamela Reed as his wife, Mary. A $.25 U.S. postage stamp honoring Hemingway was issued on the anniversary of his 90th birthday, July 21, 1989.

HEMINGWAY, Margaux   **1955-**   **Ketchum**

Model and actress Margaux Hemingway was born February 16, 1955 in Portland. She is one of three six-foot tall daughters of Jack and Byra (Puck) Hemingway and grand daughter of Ernest Hemingway. Her two sisters are Joan (Muffet) and Mariel. Her father was born in Toronto, October 9, 1923, and when his parents separated in 1926 Jack Hemingway lived with his mother, but was sent to private boarding schools, and spent summers and holidays with his father and learned to hunt and fish. Though raised in Paris he first began visiting the Ketchum-Sun Valley area in the late 1930s to hunt and fish with "Papa" and a coterie of companions that included actor Gary Cooper. Jack Hemingway entered the US Army while at Dartmouth and came out of World War II as Captain. He went to the University of Montana for a year and then back into the Army for ten years. He met his wife, Puck, the former Byra Whittlesey, daughter of a Boise drug store owner, while both were working at Sun Valley. After a career as a stock broker including several years in Portland and Eugene, Oregon in the 1950s and in the San Francisco Bay area, Jack and his family moved back to Ketchum permanently in 1967. He is an avid conservationist and served on the Idaho State Fish and Game Commission, 1970-76. Their first daughter Joan (Muffet) was born in 1950. She was a state tennis champion and later co-authored the suspense novel Rosebud (which was released as a movie in 1975) with French writer Paul Bonnecarerre.

Their second daughter, Margaux, was born February 16, 1955 in Portland. She attended Hailey High for awhile and in 1974 left for New York City. Rocky Mountain Magazine for November 1981 says:

> In 1974, the 19 year-old refugee from Hailey High School went off to New York City to see about being a model. She talked herself up in her warm husky voice, made connections and displayed an astonishing ease and versatility in front of the camera. Within months there was Margaux in Halston originals, Margaux on the cover of Vogue, Margaux in Town and Country, Margaux on the cover of Time, for Pete's sake. "The boys back home must have been short (all three sisters are six feet tall) or myopic," gushed the Time Reporter. "Margaux is the American Sex Dream incarnate, a prairie Valkyrie."
>
> ... at 20 Margaux signed the biggest advertising contract ever awarded a woman, a five year $1 million deal with Faberge to hawk Babe perfume.

Margaux has since appeared on many magazine covers and feature articles have appeared in leading magazines such as Time, Newsweek, Esquire, Vogue, New Yorker, etc. She has appeared in a number of movies and was the star of "Lipstick" produced by Paramount in 1976.

One story about the family said "Ketchum, Idaho may be the only place in the country where being a Hemingway is no big deal."

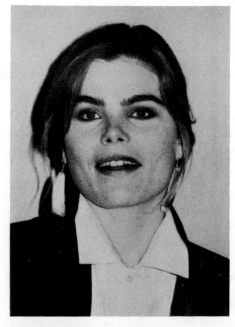

HEMINGWAY, Mariel   **1961-**   **Ketchum**

Actress Mariel Hemingway was born November 22, 1961 in San Rafael, California and raised with her sisters in Ketchum. In 1975 when her sister Margaux's face was on every newsstand, she was only thirteen and had lots of time to decide whether to be a writer, architect, or championship skier.

> Then Margaux called from New York. She was working on "Lipstick," a movie about a glamorous model who seeks vengeance after being raped. The script called for a 14-year old sister to share the heroine's ordeal. How about Mariel? At the time Mariel's previous acting experience consisted of a two-line role as the dormouse in a school production of "Alice in Wonderland."
> - <u>Rocky Mountain Magazine</u>, November 1981.

Mariel may have upstaged her sister, as the <u>New York Times</u> reviewer said "She (Mariel) gives an immensely moving, utterly unaffected performance that shows up everything else as a calculated swindle."

Mariel returned to Idaho to school and did not accept another movie role for a year and a half - that of a teen-age mother in a made-for-TV movie. She was scared in the first film but liked this one. She still wanted to finish high school but Woody Allen, fresh from the success of "Annie Hall," was looking for the right girl to play an uncomplicated 17-year old in "Manhattan." He'd seen Mariel in "Lipstick" and pried her loose from Ketchum just months before she was to graduate. Among her other movies are "Personal Best," "Star 80," and "Superman IV."

The 1981 <u>Rocky Mountain Magazine</u> article explained her desire for privacy. She doesn't ski at Sun Valley much anymore and "she even admits feeling a certain dread when she first returns to Ketchum from a film project and has to walk into Atkinson's Grocery. The shoppers are people she knows, but they are still, well, people, and they all want to know what she's been up to." Mariel has her own place in Central Idaho near Salmon now, a "two-story cabin on 22 acres of solitude," where she will have a "corner of Idaho she can call her own." She is married to Stephen Crisman and they have a daughter, Dree Louise, born December 4, 1987.

Mariel was featured on the cover of <u>TV Guide</u> (Aug. 27, 1988) and a five-page story about her career as an actress and her latest film, "Steal the Sky" in which she plays an Israeli spy.

HOBART, Kenneth C.　　　　　1961-　　　　　Kamiah

Former Kamiah High and University of Idaho quarterback Ken Hobart led the Hamilton Tiger-Cats to the Canadian Football League championship game in 1985.

Born January 27, 1961 in Cairo, Georgia, he moved with his family to Kamiah where he attended high school and lettered three years in football and four years each in baseball, basketball and track. He won All-State honors in all sports including first team quarterback, offensive back of the year, co-player of the year, most valuable player of the year, etc. in football. In basketball he was on the All-State team, MVP, and team captain. In track he won several state championships, was captain of his team and MVP, etc. for several years. The 6' 1", 185 pound athlete excelled in every sport. In baseball he was an All-State pitcher with a 40-8 win-loss record in four years. After graduation Hobart attended Lewis Clark State College for one semester in 1979 on a basketball scholarship. The "Kamiah Kid" then transferred to UI where he played quarterback for the Vandals for four seasons, 1980-83. During his career there he gained 11,126 total yards and was only the second player in NCAA history to accomplish that. Hobart set twenty-six UI, twenty-three Big Sky Conference and twelve NCAA Division I AA records. He was selected to the Division I AA All American team and his Vandal jersey, number 9, has been retired.

Hobart was a business management major at UI. When he left there, he was drafted for short stints in the USFL at Denver and then Jacksonville, Florida before signing on with the Hamilton Tiger-Cats for the Canadian Football League. In 1985 he guided his team to the Grey Cup, the Super Bowl of the CFL, and was the only unanimous selection to the Canadian East Division All Star team. Since then he has been hobbled with injuries that limited his playing time. In 1987 the "Kamiah Kid" was named quarterback of the Big Sky Conference silver anniversary team.

Hobart still keeps in touch with his former coaches including former Washington State University football's Dennis Erickson, who coached him at Idaho. And he still hopes for a chance in the National Football League.

In the fall of 1988 Hobart joined the San Diego Chargers.

HURDSTROM, Karen L.   **1934-**   **Moscow**

Another Moscow woman who became a world famous opera singer was Karen Hurdstrom. Born August 12, 1934, she attended Moscow schools, graduated from Moscow High School and obtained a B.S. in music from UI in 1956 and was Phi Beta Kappa. After receiving her M of Music in voice from Julliard School of Music in New York City in 1958 she taught singing and music history at the University of South Dakota for a year. She made her professional singing debut January 26, 1961, was named Outstanding Young Woman of America and began appearing in operas all over Europe. She returned to Moscow to open the Moscow Community Concert Series for 1965-66 in Memorial Gym. The Argonaut for October 12, 1965 fills in her career:

> The next year she joined the Robert Shaw Chorale, also doing other concerts, recordings, and T.V. performances in New York. In 1961 she received a Fullbright grant to study at the University of Cologne in Germany. After a year there, she became a student of Frau Kammersangerin Huni-Mihascek, Munich, Germany. For the past three years, she has received assistance from the Rockefeller Foundation.
>
> Miss Hurdstrom, who now lives in Vienna when she is not working in Salzberg, will sing in Cleveland, New Haven and New York before her return to Vienna.
>
> She will stay in Moscow visiting her parents until this weekend when she is going to Boise for the Utah-Idaho game, her first football game in nine years.

A few press comments early (1963) in her European career suffer a little in translation but do impress:

> The Landestheater of Salzburg brought forth the new production of "Madame Butterfly" which was for Karen Hurdstrom in the title role a great success.
>
> The artist had a beautiful, and astoundingly productive and well-trained voice. . . A beautiful first Vienna success.
>
> A coming star in singer's heaven. (Linz)
>
> It is not only the clear sure sound of her voice. . . that make it possible . . . she can become one of the great figures among European singers. (Barcelona)

Following surgery for cancer recently, Hurdstrom had to give up her opera career but still sings at weddings and high Masses. She lives in Vienna and works in the town's oldest music store. Her parents live in Moscow. Her father Al operated the Varsity Cafe there for some thirty years.

JACKSON, Lawrence Curtis   **1931–**   **Nampa/Boise**

Nampa-born Larry Jackson may have led the National League in strikeouts in 1966 but he struck out with the 1988 Idaho Legislature.

The fourteen-year major league pitcher with the Cardinals, Cubs, and Phillies and former Republican State Legislator supported Democrat Governor Cecil D. Andrus in the 1986 election and in turn was appointed by him to the State Tax Commission in 1987 (subject to the confirmation of the Idaho Senate). However, twenty-four Senate Republicans blocked the appointment. In 1989, "Andrus Republican" Jackson was appointed to the Idaho Industrial Commission, a full-time salaried position.

Jackson was born June 2, 1931 in Nampa. He started his baseball career as a right-handed pitcher with the St. Louis Cardinals in 1955, and pitched for them through 1962 when he was traded to the Chicago Cubs. Early in the 1966 season he was traded to Philadelphia.

Jackson appeared in 558 games in his major league career. His best years were with the Cubs. In 1964 he was 24-11 and led the league in wins. In 1966 he led the league in strikeouts. Although he led the National League in strikeouts in 1966 with 139, he had better years -- 145 in 1959, 148 in 1964, 153 in 1964, and 171 in 1960 -- and a career total of 1709. Not a good hitter but a pretty fair pitcher, Jackson had a career record of 194-183 and an ERA (earned run average) of 3.40. His best ERA was 2.55 in 1963.

Jackson has been in the insurance business since his retirement from baseball in 1968. In 1970 he was elected to the Idaho State House of Representatives, serving eight years until he made an unsuccessful bid for the Republican gubernatorial nomination in 1978. He served two years as chairman of the Legislative Joint Finance-Appropriations Committee.

The former-major league baseball pitcher currently lives in Garden City north of Boise and serves on the Idaho State Centennial Commission.

JENNINGS, Talbot Lanham   1894-1985   Shoshone/Nampa

Talbot Jennings was a Hollywood screen writer who wrote numerous screenplays, seventeen of which were made into movies including <u>Mutiny on the Bounty</u>, <u>Anna and the King of Siam</u>, <u>The Good Earth</u>, <u>Romeo and Juliet</u> and <u>Northwest Passage</u>.

Jennings was born in Shoshone in 1894 and moved with his family to Caldwell in 1895 and to Nampa in 1899. His father, Rev. Samuel J. Jennings, was born in Devonshire, England and educated as a mining engineer but gave up this profession for the Episcopal Church. He came to this country in the 1870s following the mines which then employed many Cornishmen. He went first to Michigan and then Butte, Montana. He left to take a church in Big Horn, Wyoming, a community settled by wealthy English cattlemen who wanted an English clergyman. Rev. Jennings also homesteaded and unwittingly employed "Butch" Cassidy and "found him reliable." He read the first civilian burial service over Custer and his men, and personally knew Buffalo Bill, Owen Wister and others. Much of the information here is from an article on Talbot Jennings in <u>Cold Drill Extra</u> published by BSU in 1984. He recalled little of grade school but:

> ... much of saddlehorse (or buckboard) and dog -- and long rides through the sagebrush over to the Snake River, fifteen miles away. I grew up then in a vast, unspoiled country of sagebrush, sky and wind, ringed about by distant mountains. During these years, I was also a tireless reader. We had a good library at home and there was also a growing town library. I entered high school in 1908. The courses then were what might be called "classical." I graduated in 1913. In summer I had a job on a railroad survey crew: chainman or stake-puncher working on branch lines which were being built through the deserts and into the mountains.

After graduation Jennings worked for the railroad as clerk, mechanic and timekeeper. He went to UI in 1915 but entered the service in WWI (1917) and was discharged as a Second Lieutenant, Field Artillery, 1919. After working for the State of Idaho for a few years he returned to UI in 1922 and received his B.A. in English in 1924. There he was ASUI President, editor of the <u>Gem of the Mountains</u> yearbook and the <u>Blue Bucket</u> magazine. He also wrote a state history set to music entitled <u>The Light on the Mountains</u> and several one-act plays. After receiving his M.A. from Harvard he returned to UI as an English instructor. In 1927 Jennings entered the Yale Drama School where he wrote plays for three major productions. He taught for a year at Miami University in Ohio and then went to New York in 1930 to try his "luck in the professional theatre." One of his plays attracted the attention of Irving Thalberg, the producer at MGM. In 1934 he went to Hollywood to write motion picture scripts for Thalberg, the first being <u>Mutiny on the Bounty</u> for Charles Laughton and Clark Gable. He spent the next thirty years in Hollywood writing screenplays. He visited UI often, donated thousands of books to the Library, was one of the founders of the friends group (Library Associates) and gave the UI commencement address in 1939, at which time he received an honorary Doctor of Literature degree. In later years he resided at East Glacier, Montana where he died June, 1985, age 89.

JEWETT, George Frederick   **1896-1956**   **Lewiston**

To Idaho's important lumber industry, George Frederick Jewett brought enlightened and capable leadership as an executive of Potlatch Forests, Inc. of Lewiston. He was connected with the firm for many years, and to a large degree, its growth and prosperity may be traced to his major role in its direction. He was chairman of its board at the time of his death, and he also exerted a vital influence in local civic affairs and in philanthropic efforts. - <u>The History of Idaho</u>.

Jewett was born August 22, 1896 in St. Paul, Minnesota, the son of Dr. James Richard Jewett, a distinguished educator and professor of Arabic at Harvard University, 1911-33. His mother was Margaret Weyerhaeuser, the daughter of Frederick Weyerhaeuser (of Niedersaulheim, Germany) who developed the Weyerhaeuser lumbering empire.

Jewett completed his public school education in the East while his father was teaching there. He then entered Harvard but his studies there were interrupted by two years in the service, in the U.S. Navy during World War I. He returned to receive a B.A. from Harvard in 1919 and an M.A. in 1922.

Jewett went to the Northwest in the early years of his career, and in 1925 became office manager of the Clearwater Timber Co. in Lewiston, a position he held until 1928. He resigned in that year to accept appointment as general manager of the Edward Rutledge Timber Co. at Coeur d'Alene. His connection with that organization continued until 1931, when the firms merged and became Potlatch Forests, Inc. He became its president in 1946, and served until 1949, when he was named chairman of the board. At the time of Mr. Jewett's death, his role of leadership in the company and in the industry was appraised by his successor in the presidency, William P. Davis. "To Mr. Jewett, PFI was his life's work," said Mr. Davis. "He was a pioneer in wise timber management, a sound practitioner of good business standards and a great humanitarian." - <u>The History of Idaho</u>.

Jewett found time in his busy schedule to serve on numerous boards of directors including those of the Northern Pacific Railroad, Columbia Electric, Spokane Branch of the Seattle First National Bank, the Air University, etc. He also belonged to the Harvard Club and New York Yacht Club. He and his wife were generous contributors and actively involved in the parish of St. John's Cathedral in Spokane where they lived from 1937-56. Jewett was a lay reader there.

Jewett contributed also to many educational institutions including the UI. The George F. Jewett papers are maintained in the UI Library Special Collections Department. He continued to serve as chairman of the board of PFI until his death November 23, 1956.

JOHNSON, Gus　　　　　**1938-87**　　　　　**BSU/UI**

Born December 13, 1938 and raised in Akron, Ohio, basketball star Gus Johnson came West and played at Boise Junior College in 1961-62 and led the Broncos to a 19-8 season before transferring to UI. Johnson played only one season, 1962-63, at UI but he set the standard for Vandal basketball with a bold style of play years ahead of his time. He was doing in the 1960s what players such as Julius Erving made commonplace in the 1980s. In one year Johnson became a legend. People started lining up at 3 in the afternoon for an evening game, to make sure they got into Memorial Gym to see Gus Johnson play.

Everyone had their Gus Johnson story. One example occurred during the game with Gonzaga. Johnson snagged a defensive rebound and started to fast break. Spotting a teammate at the other end of the court he leaped up and began a long pass. A Gonzaga defender went up and blocked the passing lane. Still in the air, Johnson pulled the ball back then whipped it behind his back three-fourths the length of the court, hitting Chuck White one step from the basket for an Idaho layup.

The Vandals finished 20-6 that year and it was another 18 years before they had another 20 win season (1981). Johnson was drafted by the NBA in 1964 and went to work for the Baltimore (later Washington) Bullets. His exceptional strength, speed, and agility led the Bullets to the playoffs five times during his 10-year NBA career. He was the Bullets first real superstar and they retired his number - 25.

Idaho was responsible for getting Johnson out of the pool halls and onto the basketball court where he belonged. After his retirement from basketball he did some TV and radio commentary in Akron, coached some at Kent State and for the Cavaliers and Pacers and most recently owned a vinyl repair shop with his younger brother Perry who played basketball at Moscow High School when Gus was a Vandal.

Johnson liked fancy things, saying he was making up for having grown up in a ghetto. He drove a custom-built Cadillac around Akron and sometimes had a great Dane at his side. Gus once owned 75 pairs of shoes. When he returned to Moscow in 1976 to play in the alumni game in celebration of the opening of the Kibbie Dome, he wore a full-length mink coat and had a gold star implanted in one of his front teeth.

In January 1987, dying of cancer, he was inducted into the BSU Athletic Hall of Fame. In April he was inducted into the North Idaho Athletic Hall of Fame and his number 43 Vandal Jersey was retired, with former Vandal Coach Wayne Anderson making the presentation to Johnson in Akron.

Gus Johnson died of a brain tumor in Akron, age 48, on April 28, 1987.

JOHNSON, Walter Perry   **1887-1946**   **Weiser**

Along with Babe Ruth, Honus Wagner and Ty Cobb, Walter "Big Train" Johnson was considered one of the greatest baseball players of all time, and he got his professional start with the Weiser baseball team.

Johnson was born November 6, 1887 in Humboldt, Kansas, the son of a farmer. In 1901 the family moved to Olinda, California, where Walter attended Fullerton Union High School.

In 1906, Johnson turned professional and signed with Tacoma of the Northwest League. The 16-year old was sent down to the Weiser team where he played for three seasons, from 1904-06, and pitched seventy-five scoreless innings and averaged fifteen strikeouts a game.

Johnson went on to play for the Washington Senators and established numerous records, with a mostly second division team, from 1907-27 and was elected to the Baseball Hall of Fame in 1936. He was considered the fastest pitcher in baseball. Following are some of his records and baseball statistics as recorded in the Biographical Dictionary of American Sports - Baseball:
- 416 wins in 21 seasons
- won 20 or more games a season twelve times
- record number of games completed - 531
- record number of strikeouts - 3947
- record number of shutouts - 113
- record number of consecutive scoreless innings - 56 in 1913
- career high number of wins - 36 in 1913
- pitched in most games in American League history - 802
- career ERA of 2.17
- led American League pitchers in strikeouts twelve seasons

"Big Train" Johnson pitched the opening game for the Senators in 1910 with President Howard Taft in attendance and thus began a tradition in Washington, D.C. Johnson is described in the Biographical Dictionary of American Sports:

> In Washington, fans quickly accepted Johnson as everybody's country cousin. A big, modest hick with a behind the plow gait, he did not fit into city ways and was amazed that people thought he was so wonderful. The country bumpkin neither smoked nor drank and lived a social life of movie-going, hunting and talking baseball...

His later career as a manager at Newark and Washington was less successful. After a season as a play-by-play radio announcer for the Senators he went back to his farm and raised cattle. He was one of the five charter members of the baseball Hall of Fame. Walter "Big Train" Johnson died of a brain tumor, December 10, 1946 in Washington, D.C., age 59.

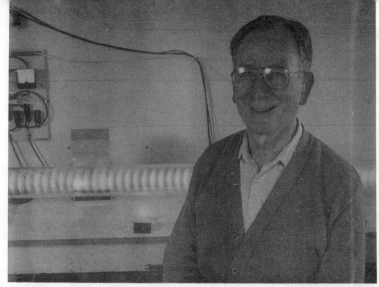

JOHNSTON, Lawrence Harding **1918-** **Moscow**

August 6, 1945, 8:16 a.m.: a pinprick of purplish-red light expands to a glowing fireball hundreds of feet wide. The temperature at its core is 50 million degrees Celsius. At "ground zero," the Shima clinic, directly beneath the detonation of the first atomic bomb on inhabited territory, the temperature reached several thousand degrees Celsius.

At a height of 29,000 feet, Larry Johnston was witnessing the first nuclear holocaust out of the porthole of the B-29 in which he was travelling. -- The Argonaut, September 20, 1983. The headlines for that story in The Argonaut read - "The man behind the trigger - UI prof invented the device that set off the atom bomb."

Larry Johnston was born February 11, 1918 in Tse-Nan-Fu, Shantung Province, China, to two American missionaries. Five years later the family returned to the U.S. Following education in the public schools, Johnston received his B.A. in 1940 and his Ph.D. in physics in 1950 from the University of California at Berkeley. He worked at the M.I.T. Radiation Laboratory from 1940-43 developing microwave radar and from 1943-45, developing the Atomic Bomb. Johnston was only twenty-three when he went to work at Los Alamos in April, 1943 and said it was an amazing experience to be working with a team of Nobel Prize winners. That team consisted of Enrico Fermi, Hans Bethe, and Ernest O. Lawrence. The A-Bomb project was directed by the controversial but brilliant J. Robert Oppenheimer.

Newsweek (July 29, 1985) featured Johnston in a 20-page article commemorating the fortieth anniversary of the dropping of the A-Bomb on Hiroshima.

Johnston later taught at the University of Minnesota from 1950-61, worked at the Aerospace Corporation in Los Angeles, from 1961-63, and the Stanford Linear Accelerator Center before coming to UI in 1967 as professor of physics. He wanted to come to Idaho for the "simple life" and to get away from the "very large complex projects."

According to an article in the Daily Idahonian (May 21-22) honoring his retirement from UI in 1988:
Johnston's last ten years at UI have been spent building a laser and studying molecules through infrared light. The UI machine shop fashioned the metal fittings for the laser, and Johnston used a 12-foot long glass tube - normally used in cheese factories to carry curds and whey - to contain the pulsing pink light. He muses: all my life they have been buying me toys to play with. So long as I can earn enough to eat, I'm happy." The small laboratory at UI is a far cry from the digs his equals enjoy at Berkeley, MIT and Stanford.

The three major historic events relating to the Atomic Bomb occurred on July 16, 1945 when it was exploded at Almagordo, NM, August 6, when it was dropped on Hiroshima, and August 9, when it was dropped on Nagasaki. Larry Johnston was present at all three.

JORDAN, Leonard Beck   **1899-1983**   **Boise**

As a rancher and businessman, Idaho State Legislator, Governor of Idaho, and Congressman, Len Jordan had a creditable record of service.

Born at Mount Pleasant, Utah, May 15, 1899, he moved with his family to Enterprise, Oregon as an infant and went to the public schools there. His college education at Utah State in Logan was interrupted in 1917 by a two-year stint in the U.S. Army during World War I. Jordan then returned to Enterprise and worked as a clerk and bookkeeper. In the fall of 1920 he entered the University of Oregon where he lettered in football, was elected to Phi Beta Kappa, and received his B.A. in 1923.

Jordan went to work for the Portland Gas and Coke Co. and later for Thurlowe Glove Co. as an accountant and office manager. In 1930 he became foreman of the Tuttle Creek Ranch of Dobbin and Huffman on the Snake river, an outfit running some 6,000 sheep. After other ranching jobs and interests he moved to Grangeville to provide further education for his children, who until then had been home-taught. Jordan purchased the J.F. Graham Insurance Co. there which he ran until 1946. At Grangeville he became active in civic affairs and was elected to the Idaho State Legislature in 1946. He won the Republican nomination and election as governor in 1950 and served one four-year term, 1951-55. At that time the Idaho Governor could not succeed himself. President Eisenhower appointed him chairman of the U.S. Section of the International Joint Commission and he served in this capacity in Washington, D.C. from 1955-57.

After resigning in August of 1957, Jordan became one of the principal owners of the Circle C Cattle Ranch, one of the largest and oldest in the State. In 1962 he was appointed to the U.S. Senate replacing the late Senator Henry C. Dworshak and served with distinction in that post until his retirement in 1972. He was succeeded by Senator James McClure.

As governor, Jordan worked hard for an improved, long-range highway program, increased emphasis on the teaching of the fundamentals in the public schools, and quality higher education.

Grace Edington, of Hood River, Oregon, whom he married in 1924, was a distinguished author in her own right and best known for the book Home Below Hell's Canyon, a family biography.

Jordan received an honorary Doctor of Laws degree from UI in 1970. He died of a stroke in Boise, June 30, 1983.

JOSEPH, Chief   **ca.1840-1904**   **Lapwai**

In 1968 the U.S. Post Office issued a 6 cent stamp honoring the American Indian. This stamp depicts Chief Joseph "In tribute to the Nez Perce (pierced nose) chief and his people." Only two other Idahoans are depicted on a U.S. postage stamp - Philo Farnsworth in 1983, and Ernest Hemingway in 1989.

<u>The American Academic Encyclopedia says</u>:

Chief Joseph, c. 1840-1904, was a chief of the Nez Perce Indian tribe. He is remembered principally for his leadership during the hostilities that broke out between the U.S. Army and the Nez Perce in 1877. Friendly with the whites until then, the Nez Perce had once occupied much territory in the region where Washington, Oregon and Idaho adjoin. Under the terms of the Stevens Treaty of 1855, the Nez Perce agreed to cede much of their land to the U.S. government in return for the guarantee of a large reservation in Oregon and Idaho. When gold was discovered in Oregon in 1863, however, the government demanded that the Nez Perce relinquish this part of the reservation also. Chief Joseph resisted but later agreed to move peacefully with his people to the Lapwai Reservation in Idaho.

Fighting broke out in 1877 when young Nez Perce warriors retaliated for what they considered outrageous acts by the white settlers. In the war that followed, Joseph showed remarkable skills in military tactics by defeating larger U.S. forces in several battles. He then led his people on a retreat of more than a thousand miles over mountainous terrain in an effort to reach Canada. On September 30, 1877, however, Federal troops overtook the Nez Perce only 30 miles from the border.

With most of his warriors dead or wounded and his people starving, Chief Joseph surrendered saying "I will fight no more forever." Some historians say Joseph was only a spiritual leader and that he is given too much credit for his military tactics (some called him "the Indian Napolean"). Rafe Gibbs, in his history of Idaho entitled <u>Beckoning the Bold</u>, describes Joseph as "a gentle and kind man with handsome and serene features, emerged as the war leader..." and was inclined to "take the word of the late, unforgettable General Edward R. Chrisman in ROTC lectures at the University of Idaho" who said:

Chief Joseph led what is perhaps the most masterful fighting retreat in the history of warfare. The U.S. Armed Forces don't believe in retreating, but, in case you ever have to do so, remember Chief Joseph.

Sent to Indian Territory in Oklahoma, the Nez Perce were finally allowed to return to Idaho in 1883-84. Chief Joseph died on the Colville Indian Reservation in Washington, September 21, 1904. The cause of death, according to the doctor, was heartbreak. His grave, northeast of Nespelem, is a tourist site.

PHOTO: Adversaries - General Howard and Chief Joseph.

JUVE, Henrik (Hank)   **1899-**   **Moscow**

Time-Life Books (Vol. VII) entitled <u>This Fabulous Century</u> ranked Juve along with Jules Verne and H.G. Wells in a listing of the top science fiction writers. "Hank" was a familiar face around Moscow and the UI campus where he worked as an electrician for the Physical Plant for some twenty-two years. But few if any knew of his previous career as a science fiction writer of note. We could tell he knew a lot about electronics though.

Henrik Dahl Juve was born August 29, 1899 in Neilsville, Wisconsin, (the oldest of six sons) and moved with his family in 1912 to Enterprise, Oregon where he attended public schools. Later Juve attended Willamette University in Salem and the University of Washington in Seattle, majoring in electrical engineering. He worked for Pacific Gas and Electric until 1924 when he returned to Enterprise.

During the early years of the depression, when science fiction was just beginning to be printed in popular magazines, Juve began writing his stories by day while working as a projectionist in a theater at night. In 1937 he moved to Moscow and taught in the Naval Training School on campus during World War II. Afterwards he worked at UI as an electrician until his retirement in 1966.

His first story entitled "The Silent Destroyer," was published by Hugo Gernsback in <u>Air Wonder Stories</u> magazine (August 1929) and won acclaim among science-fiction buffs. It tells of a device called "A molecular disrupter," which today we call a laser beam. Time-Life Books credits Juve with being the first to describe a laser-like device. In an article in the <u>Idahonian</u> for June 5, 1984, Juve's career as a science-fiction writer is related and states:

> In 1960, some thirty years after he (Juve) first wrote about it, a scientist at Hughes Aircraft Corporation in California developed the first practical laser instrument.

Over a period of four years his stories appeared regularly in <u>Science Wonder Stories</u>, <u>Wonder Stories Quarterly</u>, and <u>Wonder Stories</u>. An anthology of Juve's stories has been placed in the UI Library Special Collections Department. Juve wrote about such things as television, radar, quartz-clocks, artificial food pills, instant cameras, computers, tape recorders, infra-red and ultralight rays, transmutation, anti-sleep pills, and anti-gravity, in some cases long before they were invented. Asked about Hank's writing, his daughter, Donna Marie, said he always read and admired inventors like Tesla. A good physics text was good reading to him, and he always started writing with a plain sheet of paper and let his characters take over the story. The Spring, 1989 issue of <u>Extrapolation</u> (Kent State U. Press) has a 47-page article entitled "Henrik Dahl Juve and the Second Gernsback Dynasty." It gives some story summaries and includes sample correspondence between the author and his editor/publisher.

Hank Juve still lives in Moscow and his son, Henrik Juve, Jr. is a professor of Chemistry at UI.

KILLEBREW, Harmon Clayton   **1936-**   **Payette**

Baseball's premier home-run hitter in the 1960's and 1970's was from Payette.
<u>Current Biography</u> (1966) says:

> Major-league baseball's leading challenger of Babe Ruth's lifetime home-run average
> (11.8) is Harmon Killebrew of the Minnesota Twins, who entered the 1966 season
> with a record of one homer for every 12.6 times at bat. Killebrew, who joined
> the Twins in 1954 (when they were the Washington Senators) did not become a regular
> in the starting lineup until 1959, has a big-league total of 194 home runs. While
> eleven other players have higher totals, none goes the full circuit with as
> great frequency, and none, with the possible exception of Mickey Mantle, hits the
> ball farther.

Born June 29, 1936 in Payette, Killebrew played varsity baseball, basketball and football as a freshman at
Payette High School and lettered in each sport annually. After high school he enrolled at the College of
Idaho and while playing semi-pro baseball in the Idaho-Oregon Border League, Killebrew terrified
opponents with an .847 batting average (.300 is pretty good). He was scouted by four different major
league teams. After the Washington Senators scout watched Harmon belt out four home runs, three
triples and four other hits in twelve times at bat, he signed Harmon to a $30,000 contract - $6,000 a year
for three years and a $12,000 bonus -- in 1954.

His first years in the majors were not too successful but with time and tutelage he came on in 1959 as
the slugging sensation of the American League. In one stretch Killebrew hit eight homers in twelve days.
In 1960 the Washington franchise was moved to Minneapolis-St. Paul where the team became the
Minnesota Twins. With a new organization, Killebrew had a slump in the first half of the 1960 season,
hitting only four homers. He spurted in the second half of the season and ended up with thirty-one. In
1961 he boosted his home-run tally to forty-six which normally might have earned him the league
leadership, but 1961 was not a normal year. Roger Maris of the New York Yankees hit sixty-one homers
and teammate Mickey Mantle hit fifty-four so Killebrew's achievement went unnoticed except in
Minnesota. In 1962 he led the American League with forty-eight home runs and 126 runs-batted-in. He
also won the home run crown in 1963 and 1964.

Harmon (Killer) Killebrew was the premier home run hitter of the majors during the 1960's and 1970's,
leading the American League in this category six times. He ended his twenty-two year career in the
majors with 573 career homers and his number, 3, was retired by the Twins. Since his retirement in
1975, he announced Twins baseball games. Driving through Payette you can't miss Killebrew Stadium.

KING, Carole   **1941-**   **Custer Co.**

Idahoans are probably most familiar with Carole King's private ranch road in Custer County but she has actually had a very successful career for over twenty years as a singer/song writer in the world of pop music. She has a new album called "City Streets" (Capitol), 1989.

Her real name is Carole Klein and her biographical sketch in <u>Current Biography</u> (1974) says:
> Carole King was born in Brooklyn, New York on February 9, 1941 to middle-class
> parents. Her father, an insurance salesman, was formerly a fireman; her mother was
> a public school teacher. After graduating from Madison High School in Brooklyn,
> Carole enrolled at Queens College, where her classmates included Neil Diamond and
> Paul Simon. She dropped out of college after her freshman year (age 17) to marry Gerry
> Goffin, a laboratory assistant and aspiring chemist who shared her interest in popular music.

The <u>Rolling Stone Encyclopedia of Rock and Roll</u> says of her:
> Singer/songwriter Carole King has had two outstanding careers. Throughout
> the Sixties, she was one of pop's most prolific songwriters, writing
> the music to songs like "Will You Love Me Tomorrow?" and "Up on the Roof,"
> with most lyrics by her first husband, Gerry Goffin. Then in 1971, with her
> multimillion-selling "Tapestry," she helped inaugurate the Seventies' singer/
> songwriter style.

King began studying and playing piano at four. "An intellectually precocious teenager, she started a female vocal ensemble in school under a trigonometrical name, Co-sines." She was a childhood friend of Neal Sedaka and he wrote a hit song called "Oh! Carol," in 1959, dedicated to her. In 1961, she and Goffin co-wrote "Will you Love Me Tomorrow?" They wrote over 100 hits together. In the late Sixties, King formed her own group, wrote her own lyrics, and recorded solo. She divorced Goffin and temporarily was married to Charles Larkey. She later married Rick Evers, her collaborator at the time, but he died of a heroin overdose in 1978.

She then married Rick Sorenson and "they just wanted some privacy and a little peace when they paid $1 million for the historic Robinson Bar Ranch in 1981. They've been front page news ever since."
<u>Lewiston Tribune</u>, October 19, 1987.
> When the Sorensons moved to their 117-acre ranch, tucked along the Salmon River,
> in the Sawtooth National Recreation Area east of Sunbeam, Idaho, they locked a
> gate across a (.8 mile) winding dirt road that had been used by locals for years.

The ranch once belonged to Governor Chase A. Clark. In 1988 the Idaho Supreme Court ruled the road is private and Carole could lock her gate.

KRAMER, Jerry   **1936-**   **Sandpoint**

Former Green Bay Packer football star Gerald Louis (Jerry) Kramer grew up in Sandpoint and played football at UI. In 1969 he was voted the outstanding guard in the history of professional football. Born January 23, 1936 in Jordan, Montana (@ 83 miles NW of Miles City, in Eastern Montana - pop. 485 in 1980), Jerry Kramer moved with his family to Sandpoint where he grew up and attended high school. He played football there as a tackle and placekicker. Kramer played football at UI from 1955-58 and track, 1956-57. In his senior year the UI business administration major was selected to play in the East-West Shrine game, and captained the West team. He also played in the North-South post-season game.

According to the Biographical Dictionary of American Sports:

At 6 feet, 3 inches, 250 pounds, Kramer was drafted by the Green Bay Packers as a guard in the fourth round of the 1958 NFL, draft and teamed with Fred Thurston to give the Packers among the games best set of guards. In 1961 he missed eight games because of a broken ankle. Besides playing guard full-time in 1962, he later became the Packers' placekicker when Paul Hornung injured his knee. Kramer made 9 of 11 field goal attempts and 38 of 39 extra points for 65 total points. He capped the season by kicking three field goals and one extra point in Green Bay's 16-7 win over the New York Giants for the NFL Championship.

Against Dallas in the 1967 NFL title game, Kramer threw the crucial block on the Cowboys' Jethro Pugh, allowing quarterback Bart Starr to score the winning touchdown for the Packer's third straight championship. Kramer appeared with Green Bay in the first two Super Bowls, won by the Packers. Before retiring in 1968, he played on five championship teams (1961-1962, 1965-1967), was named All-Pro five times (1960, 1962-63, 1966-67), and participated in three Pro Bowls (1962-63, 1968).

Kramer has lectured around the country and written a number of books including: Instant Replay: The Green Bay Diary of Jerry Kramer (1968); Farewell to Football (1969); Distant Replay (1985); and Lombardi (1986).

Jerry Kramer lived for a time in Boise after he retired from football.

LAW, Vernon   **1930-**   **Meridian**

Meridian's Vern Law became a major league baseball pitcher for the Pittsburgh Pirates, won the Cy Young Award, and two of the four World Series games won by his team against the New York Yankees in 1960.

> Vernon Sanders Law was born March 12, 1930 in Meridian, Idaho, the second of three sons born to Jesse Law, a farmer and mechanic, and Melva C. (Sanders) Law. Jesse Law had ten children by his first wife, who left him a widower. Vern's two brothers are Evan and Erin Dennis. He grew up in Meridian and attended the local high school, where he played in the band, sang in the chorus, and won twelve letters in baseball, basketball, and football. After his graduation in 1948, Vern went on to study vocational cabinetmaking at Boise Junior College at Boise, Idaho. - Current Biography, 1961.

Law came to the attention of the Pirates when Senator Herman Welker of Idaho saw him play and called his former Gonzaga classmate Bing Crosby, one of the Pirates owners. Law was about to sign with the Brooklyn Dodgers when his mother received a call from the crooner himself and Bing convinced her that young Vernon should sign instead with the Pirates.

Law played in the minor leagues at Santa Rosa, Davenport and New Orleans before moving up to the Pirates in 1950. He spent 1951-53 in the U.S. Army and returned to the Pirates in 1954. The turning point in his career was 1958 when he helped lead the previously last-place Pirates into second place in the National League. Law finished the 1959 season with an 18-9 record and a 2.98 earned run average. In 1960 he won eight of his first nine starts and led the Pirates to the National League pennant with a 20-9 won-lost record. He was chosen to the All-Star team and was the starting pitcher for the National League in the All-Star game. Law was nicknamed "the deacon" by his team mates, out of respect for his Mormon faith. Actually he was an elder, qualified to baptize, marry and perform related sacraments. He did not pitch on Sunday but instead would preach at the local church wherever he happened to be playing. The six foot three inch, two hundred pound pitcher practiced what he preached. He neither smoked nor drank and according to Current Biography:

> ...the strongest oath he has ever been heard to utter is "Judas Priest." He fasts once a month, giving the money he saved on food to missionaries, and he allots one-tenth of his salary, now estimated at $30,000 (1961) to his church.

Vernon Law retired from baseball in 1967, after pitching for 16 seasons, and became a coach for the Pirates in 1968.

LAWYER, Chief   **1796-1876**   **Lapwai**

The Nez Perce were always friendly to the white man. When Lewis and Clark came through what is now the State of Idaho they were met and assisted by Chief Twisted Hair of the Nez Perce Indians. He was the father of another famous Nez Perce Chief, Hallahotsoot, called Lawyer by the mountain men because of his argumentative disposition and general shrewdness. Lawyer was the head chief of the Nez Perce from the mid to late 1800's and negotiated and signed the Treaties of 1855 and 1863 with the U.S. government. According to Rafe Gibbs in <u>Beckoning the Bold</u>, Chief Lawyer was given his name by the whites "because of his speechmaking ability, and who in later life enhanced his courtly role by wearing a silk top hat." His full name was Archie B. Lawyer.

Lawyer accepted the Treaty in 1855 with the Government because it left the Indians with most of the land they had always lived on. But Congress did not vote on the treaty right away and when the miners came into the Nez Perce lands during the gold rush, starting in 1860 when Captain Elias Pierce discovered gold along a tributary of the Clearwater, the U.S. government did not protect the Indians' rights. Instead they made the Nez Perce accept a much smaller reservation in the Treaty of 1863.
The article on Chief Lawyer in Beal and Wells <u>History of Idaho</u> says:

> He was not only a Nez Perce Chief but an ordained minister and was often
> called Reverend Lawyer ... he went to Oklahoma Indian Territory where
> Chief Joseph and the Nez Perce Indian prisoners were being held. On three
> different occasions Archie B. Lawyer accompanied Chief Joseph to Washington,
> D.C. to make pleas for the return of the captives.
> Archie Lawyer became one of the first pupils of Sue McBeth, Presbyterian
> missionary to the Nez Perce, and was ordained by the church on her
> recommendation. When he returned from the national capitol, he assumed
> the ministership of the Presbyterian Church at Spalding, on the Reservation.
> Later he was the first minister of the Second Presbyterian Church at Kamiah in
> the Lewis County section of the Reservation.

Lawyer died at Kamiah in 1876, before the Nez Perce War started. Lawyer Canyon State Park near Craigmont is named after him. Mylie Lawyer, a great granddaughter, still lives in Lapwai.

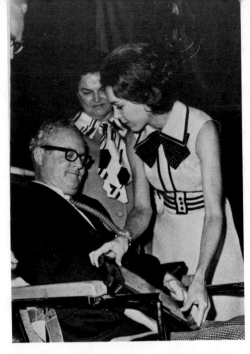

LIND, (Fearless) Farris   1915-1983   Twin Falls/Boise

"Fearless Farris," the Stinker Stations owner, was born November 8, 1915 in Twin Falls. Fascinated with airplanes and flying, he did farm work as a teenager to finance his interest and obtain his pilot's license. After high school he worked in theater management, then in radio promotion for Texaco in Canada and Conoco in Denver.

In 1939 Lind married and developed a petroleum products brokerage business in Butte. Then he moved to Boise and established the Fearless Farris Cut Rate Gasoline Stations. During World War II he was a Navy fighter pilot instructor. After the war he did crop dusting but mainly he expanded his chain of Fearless Farris Stinker Stations all over the West. His road signs provided some laughs along the desolate stretches of highway and attracted tourists to his stations. A few examples were:

> If your wife wants to drive don't stand in her way.
> Sheepherders headed for town have the right of way.
> Don't just sit there, nag your husband.
> Tourists must not laugh at natives.
> Sage brush is free - take some home to your mother-in-law.
> Warning Methodists - watch out for Mormon crickets.
> Nudist area - keep your eyes on the road.
> If you lived here, you'd be home now.
> Sitting Bull stood up here.

Lind got his nickname "Fearless" because he was a fearless challenger to the major oil companies and used the skunk-stinker logo because his competition said he was a "stinker" to deal with. Upon taking oral polio vaccine with his family in 1963, when the program was being urged on all citizens to stamp out polio, he was stricken with the disease and paralyzed from the neck down. Although he spent the last twenty years of his life in an iron lung or attached to a mechanical breathing device, he refused to give up. Bedfast for twenty years, he directed and expanded his business, hiring as many as two hundred people at times. His powerful will and strong spirit were an inspiration to many.

His courage and spirit caused the President of the U.S. to fly him to Washington, D.C. for a special three-day ceremony at the White House and on May 2, 1973 he was presented with the "Outstanding Handicapped Citizen's Award" by Julie Nixon, on behalf of her father. Fearless Farris died January 12, 1983, age 67 at his residence in Cascade.

LINDLEY, Ernest K.   **1899-1979**   **Moscow**

The son of Ernest Hiram Lindley, UI President, 1912-20, a distinguished author, Washington news correspondent and news analyst. Ernest Kidder Lindley was born July 14, 1899 in Richmond, Indiana. He studied at the University of Kansas and then the University of Indiana (1916-17) but his education was interrupted by World War I, during which he served as a second lieutenant in the U.S. Army. Current Biography (1943) states:

> At the end of the War he entered the University of Idaho and received his B.A. degree in 1920. During his college years he had won his Phi Beta Kappa key and had shown such ability that he was given a Rhodes scholarship upon his graduation. He spent the next three years at Oxford, specializing in economics and modern history. In 1923 he received his English B.A. with honors.

Lindley began his newspaper career the following year with the Wichita (Kansas) Beacon and later that year joined the staff of the New York World. During the Presidential campaign of 1928 he toured with both Alfred E. Smith and Herbert Hoover. When told to cover Hoover's inauguration, he went instead to the inauguration of N.Y. Governor Franklin D. Roosevelt because "Lindley's political acumen showed him a man destined to occupy the White House." In 1931, a short time before FDR opened his presidential campaign, Lindley wrote his first book entitled Franklin D. Roosevelt; a Career in Progressive Democracy. It was the first and only full-sized biography of FDR and was received very favorably. Lindley then joined the New York Herald Tribune. When FDR took office Lindley's stock rose immeasurably, and he was sent to Washington, as Newsweek said, as "reporter-confidant extraordinary of the new Administration." Lindley wrote two other books on the Roosevelt Administration and in 1937 became Washington correspondent for Newsweek and chief of their Washington Bureau. Lindley knew important personalities intimately and continued to write books and numerous articles on national and international politics. He wrote syndicated columns for the Washington Post and other newspapers and was a State Department consultant during the Kennedy Administration. Current Biography quotes Newsweek publisher Malcolm Muir as follows:

> Lindley is a rare combination of ferret and owl, of lively intellectual curiosity and extraordinary intellectual detachment. As his colleagues will tell you, he is closest of them all to the key figures of the Administration. Yet there has never been a suggestion that his personal proximity interferes with ... his job of reporting the facts to the nation.

The six foot, slim brown-eyed and brown-haired Lindley also served two years as editor of the UI Argonaut, and received an honorary Doctor of Literature degree from UI in 1960. He died June 30, 1979 in Washington, D.C.

LYNN, Judy   **1936-**   **Boise**

The 1955 Miss Idaho went on to become a famous country western singing and recording star. Judy Lynn Voiten was born April 12, 1936 in Boise and attended Franklin High. She was chosen Queen of the Snake River Stampede in 1952, and Miss Idaho in 1955 and was a runner-up Miss America in 1956 to Lee Ann Meriwether.

In 1955 she was also chosen as Billboard's Most Promising Female Country Vocalist and Pioneer magazine's Best-dressed Female Vocalist, as noted in The Country Music Encyclopedia (1974). Judy Lynn went on to a successful career that spanned the years from 1956-80. She married promoter Jack Kelly in 1956 and went to the Grand Ole Opry and was "on the road" for twenty five years. Judy Lynn (no relation to Loretta) toured with Gene Autry, Eddy Arnold, Rex Allen, Eddie Fisher, and Elvis Presley, among others. She was co-host with Ernest Tubbs on the first coast-to-coast Grand Ole Opry Show.

Judy was interviewed by Cold Drill Extra (BSU) in 1984 and Janie Pavlic reported:
> From the moment she opened her parent's front door I felt awash in the warmth
> and graciousness that emanates from Judy Lynn.
> Admittedly I was startled to see that she looks nothing like the photos
> I'd seen from her country singing heyday. Her long, honey-colored hair
> is now worn up and her unadorned face is framed by glasses.
> (asked about the highlight of her career, Judy replied)
> The most exciting part was playing in Nashville. I had a hard time getting started
> in show business. I felt rejected. I have a kind of Peggy Lee-type
> voice, what's called a "cross-over voice." It wasn't easily accepted in
> the beginning and I felt rejected. Tommy Jackson said my singing was "not
> country." Then, 15 years later, at the Close-Out of the Colonel Luncheon
> with Johnny Cash, I got a standing ovation and it healed all my wounds.

Of Idaho, Judy Lynn said "There's not a greater place to be born. I skied, played tennis, golfed, mainly individual sports. And horses ... I mainly rode by myself ... I remember snow and fun ... sledding ... and the irrigation ditches ... we swam in the canals and chased water skippers."

Judy Lynn also said in this interview that they "bought land in Oklahoma, 120 acres, when I quit show business in 1980 ... Eventually though, I'm confident that we'll move back to Idaho."

MAXEY, David R.   **1936-84**   **Boise**

Boise-born, UI alum David R. Maxey became a distinguished journalist and editor of <u>Look</u> magazine and <u>GEO</u>.

David Roy Maxey was written up in <u>Contemporary Authors</u>. His sketch is in volume 73/76 and his obituary notice in volume 112 says:

> Born October 22, 1936, in Boise, Idaho; died of cancer, April 19, 1984.
> Editor and journalist. Maxey joined the staff of <u>Look</u> magazine in 1961
> as an assistant editor, and by 1971, when the magazine ceased publication,
> he was managing editor. He subsequently served as an editor for <u>Psychology
> Today</u> and <u>Sports Afield</u> and as a staff writer for <u>Life</u>. In 1980 Maxey
> became a contributing editor to Knapp Communications Corporation, later
> serving as managing editor and then as editor of <u>Geo</u> magazine. At the
> time of his death he was corporate vice-president of Knapp. In addition
> to many articles he wrote for magazines, Maxey contributed to the 1972
> <u>Encyclopedia Britannica</u> Book of the Year.

Among his more notable assignments as a journalist and free-lance writer were the coverage of the Apollo 8 and Apollo 11 moonshots, the assassination of Robert Kennedy, the 1972 U.S. presidential election, <u>Life</u> stories on Bella Abzug and George Wallace, and <u>Psychology Today</u> interview with Walter Mondale.

Following his B.S. in 1958 from UI Maxey served in the United States Army (artillery) from 1959-60 and became a second lieutenant. He received an MBA from Harvard in 1961. Maxey majored in business administration at UI. In addition to serving as ASUI President, he was a member of the Beta Theta Phi fraternity and was named one of the top ten seniors to graduate in 1958. In late October, 1983 he returned to the UI campus to attend a class reunion and serve as grand marshall of the annual homecoming parade.

About editing a magazine, Maxey said "My job is similar to that of a ringmaster in a circus. The average day is a series of 100 two or three-minute conversations with various staff members, writers, or photographers." Looking back on his extracurricular activities, Maxey said his job as ASUI President provided a valuable experience that helped him later in life: "The job forced you to listen, which is an awfully good thing to be able to do," he said. "We really don't have enough good listeners."

MCCLURE, Sen. James Albertus   1924-   **Payette**

Idaho's senior senator was born December 27, 1924 in Payette. After attending Payette public schools, James A. McClure attended Idaho State University, participating in the Navy V-12 program there in the early 1940's.

After his Navy service, McClure attended the UI and obtained his Law degree in 1950. For sixteen years he practiced law with his father in Payette specializing in land, water and reclamation law. He also served as Payette City Attorney and Payette County prosecuting attorney.

In 1960 McClure was elected to the Idaho Senate and served until 1966. He was majority leader 1965-66. In 1966 he was elected to the U.S House of Representatives and in 1972 to the U.S. Senate, where he is now serving his third term.

Senator McClure is a member of the Senate Appropriations Committee and is the ranking Republican member of its subcommittee on Interior and Related Agencies. He is also the ranking Republican member of the Senate Energy and Natural Resources Committee and has served as its chairman. He is chairman of the Senate Steering Committee and a member of the Senate Rules Committee, the Senate Select Committee on Secret Military Assistance to Iran and the Nicaraguan Opposition, and the Commission on Security and Cooperation in Europe.

McClure has a home at McCall and an office at 361 Dirksen Senate Office Building in Washington, D.C.

In 1981 he received an honorary Doctor of Laws degree from UI and presently serves, along with Phillip Habib and J.R. Simplot, as Honorary Co-Chairman of the UI Centennial Campaign.

Among the numerous awards he has received as a Congressman are:
      Watchdog of Treasury Award, National Association of Businessmen
      Distinguished Service Award, National Energy Resources Org., 1982
      Leadership Award, Coalition for Peace through Strength, 1982-83
      Outstanding Legislator of the Year, National Association of Towns Township, 1983
      Leadership Award, Americans for Energy Independence, 1983
McClure was the UI's second Founders Day Award recipient, January 1989.

MCCONNELL, William J.   1839-1925   Moscow

Idaho pioneer, Governor, U.S. Senator and member of the Constitutional Convention (1890), William J. McConnell was born September 18, 1839 in Commerce, Michigan. He was educated in the public schools in Michigan and:

> At the age of 21, William J. McConnell signed on as a driver with a wagon train carrying freight to the western frontier. He spent some years mining and teaching school in California and Oregon before coming to the gold mines on the Payette River in the Idaho Territory.
>
> He and a friend selected land near the town of Horseshoe Bend on which they grew fruits and vegetables to sell to the miners. This proved to be a lucrative venture for a while, but eventually the ranch became a target for horse thieves.
>
> McConnell moved to Yamhill, Oregon in 1867 and married a young lady named Louisa Brown. There he opened a general merchandise store, taught school and served on the school board. He served two terms as Oregon State senator, as a Republican. The Republican Party offered him the candidacy of Governor of Oregon for the 1878 election but he declined. - Daily Idahonian July 4, 1987.

There is a story that when McConnell first came to Idaho he walked from Oregon to Boise City. In 1878 McConnell came to Moscow and opened up a general merchandise store on the corner of Main and First. The business flourished until the depression of 1893. McConnell participated in the 1890 Constitutional Convention for the State of Idaho and drew the short term of U.S. Senator 1890-91. He was the third Governor of Idaho, 1893-96, and his daughter Mary (Mamie) McConnell accompanied him to Boise as part-time secretary and was courted by, and later married, a successful young attorney named William E. Borah.

After his second term as Governor, McConnell was appointed U.S. Indian Inspector and in 1909 President Taft commissioned him Inspector in the Immigration Service and he served until his death in 1925. McConnell wrote several books: Early History of Moscow in 1926 and Frontier Law; A Story of Vigilante Days in 1926. The McConnell Mansion in Moscow is listed on the National Historic Record and serves as headquarters for the Latah County Historical Society. McConnell served as a Regent for the University of Idaho and was awarded UI's first honorary degree, in 1894. He died March 29, 1925.

MCKENNA, Richard (Milton)   **1913-64**   **Mountain Home**

The powerful and spectacular Twentieth Century-Fox motion picture "Sand Pebbles" starring Steve McQueen, Richard Crenna, Richard Atenborough and Candice Bergen was based on a book written by Richard McKenna of Mountain Home. McKenna was born May 9, 1913 and raised in Mountain Home, where he attended public schools. In 1931, he joined the Navy and served twenty-two years until his retirement in 1953 as chief machinist's mate. He returned to college at the age of 40 and received his B.A. from the University of North Carolina in 1956. In January of that year he married Eva Mae Grice, a librarian, who became his researcher.

Sand Pebbles, his first book, published by Harper in 1962, was a Book-of-the-Month selection and won the Sir Walter Raleigh Award and the Harper Prize in 1963. Contemporary Authors says of him:
>Richard McKenna joined the Navy at the age of 18 and served for some
>twenty-two years. Ten of those years were spent in the Far East, and
>another two years on a Yangtze River gunboat in China. McKenna's experiences
>in the Navy are fictionalized in The Sand Pebbles. Telling the story of
>the crew of the Naval ship "San Pablo," which patrolled China between 1925
>and 1927, Sand Pebbles was described by R.A. Davis of Library Journal as
>"a realistic depiction of naval life (and) very well written." "If a
>novel of recent history should convey a feeling of great events." H.S. Hayward
>wrote in the Christian Science Monitor, "this one does." Granville Hicks of
>Saturday Review felt the book was the work of an "inspired amateur."

McKenna published a few short stories before Sand Pebbles and one, "The Secret Place," published posthumously, won the Nebula Award of the Science Fiction Writers of America. He had returned to Idaho in July of 1963 and began work on his second book, Sons of Martha and Other Stories. It was similar to Sand Pebbles in that it concerns a Navy ship in the prewar days of the 1930s. It was published posthumously.

As a young boy McKenna was an avid reader and user of the Mountain Home Library. He often talked about the Carnegie Library there and sent money for book purchases. In a 1962 letter to the librarian he wrote: "I am happy to have a chance to pay tribute to the Mountain Home Carnegie Library. It will always remain one of my most pleasant memories from the days I lived in Mountain Home." Mckenna died of a heart attack while working on his second book, November 1, 1964.

MCMANUS, Patrick Francis   **1933-**   **Sandpoint**

"The effect I'm after is not to convey ideas. It's to give people the emotional experience they get from laughing," said Patrick F. McManus, author of all those funny books about ill-fated outdoor excursions. - Lewiston Tribune, November 20, 1987. The outdoor humor writer who was born August 26, 1933 in Sandpoint and lived for many years in Spokane was in Lewiston signing copies of his latest book Rubber Legs and White Tail-Hairs when interviewed by a Tribune reporter.

McManus received his B.A. in 1956 and his M.A. in 1962 from Washington State University. He worked as a reporter for the Daily Olympian in 1956 and as an editor at W.S.U. from 1956-59 and was a member of the faculty at Eastern Washington University from 1959-82. He also worked as a news reporter for KREM-TV in Spokane, was Associate Editor of Field and Stream, 1976-81, editor-at-large for Outdoor Life since 1981. His books include They Shoot Canoes, Don't They? (1981), Kid Camping from Aaaaiii! to Zip (1979), and A fine and Pleasant Misery (1978). Two later books, Never Sniff a Gift Fish and The Grasshopper Trap hit the N.Y. Times best-seller list.

In his biographical sketch in Contemporary Authors, McManus is quoted:
> James Thurber once wrote that the writer of short humor pieces sits on the edge of the chair of literature. I suspect the short-humor writer roosts on one of the lower rungs, if he is allowed near the chair at all. Critics do not regard humor writing as serious literary work, which is good. As soon as the humor writer starts thinking of himself as a person of letters, as soon as he perceives his purpose as something other than seeking the ultimate, base, vulgar, gut-busting, psyche-wrenching laugh, he is done for.

McManus has lived most of what he describes in his books about calamitous camping trips and disastrous hunting and fishing expeditions and most of his characters are based on real people. The Tribune interview states:
> Each time McManus writes a new book, his previous ones start selling again, he said. His first book made the best-seller list seven years after it was published. McManus said he already has enough stories for another book. He said he might get involved in films. A young screenwriter in California is working on a script, he said, and another man is working on an animated film based on McManus' stories.

McManus and his wife Darlene have a place on Lake Pend Orielle.

MILLER, Julius Sumner   1909-87   **Moscow/UI**

A renowned physicist, teacher, and educational critic Julius Miller, became known to millions on television as "Professor Wonderful."

Born in 1909 in Billercia, Mass., Miller grew up in a hard-working farming family and loved to read. By the time he was 16 he had "read the town library dry." Miller graduated from Boston University with degrees in philosophy and theoretical physics during the Depression. Failing to find a teaching position he and his wife, Alice, became butler and maid for a wealthy Boston doctor earning $30 a month. He wrote 700 letters before landing his first teaching job at a private school in Connecticut. Miller obtained a fellowship at UI and a master's degree in physics there in 1940.

In WWII he was a U.S. Army Signal Corps civilian physicist. In 1950 he went to the Institute for Advanced Physics in Princeton, N.J. and became a friend and student of his idol, Albert Einstein. Miller amassed a collection of Einstein memorabilia that included a copy of Einstein's birth certificate.

He taught for a time at UCLA then opted for the smaller El Camino College in Torrance where he taught for 22 years, "retiring" in 1974. He continued to spend his life promoting the popular understanding of physics, in ways that audiences will never forget.

Miller used showmanship to hook people on the basic principles of a field that can be frightening to the uninitiated. In the classroom he used to shout, leap and wave his arms. His favorite audiences were children. He appeared on hundreds of TV shows and was known on TV as "Professor Wonderful" to millions of children in the 1950s and 1960s, on "The Mickey Mouse Club" program and was a guest on television talk shows of Johnny Carson, Steve Allen, Mike Douglas, Art Linkletter, and Groucho Marx. In the course of his long association with Walt Disney he served as technical consultant for such Disney movies as The Absent Minded Professor, Son of Flubber and the Million Dollar Duck. Some of his greatest successes were in Australia which he visited more than 20 times. He published several books and over 300 articles in professional journals.

Miller is a member of the UI Alumni Hall of Fame. In 1971 he was named Outstanding Educator in America. In 1984 the American Association of Physics Teachers cited Miller "for extraordinary service in bringing physics to the public and to the physics teaching community for over 50 years." In 1985 he appeared at the UI to a packed audience.

"Professor Wonderful" died of leukemia April 14, 1987, age 78, at his home in Torrance, CA.

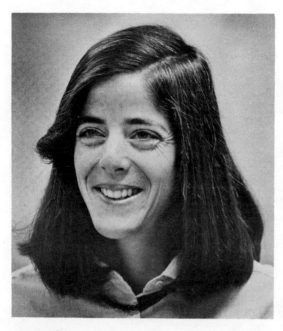

MORGAN, Barbara   **1951-**   **McCall**

Idaho's NASA Teacher in Space, Barbara Morgan, was born, raised and educated in California and teaches third grade in McCall. She was selected as one of ten finalists for the Teacher in Space Program in 1984 out of over 11,000 teacher applicants. She was back up for Christa McAuliffe and they began six months of intensive pre-flight training at Johnson Space Center in Houston, Texas in 1985. After the Challenger tragedy on January 28, 1986, in which Christa McAuliffe died, Barbara was given the opportunity to carry on and she never wavered.

Following are some excerpts from an article about Barbara Morgan in the Summer, 1987 issue of Central Idaho:

> At 36 years of age Barbara is a small wiry woman with merry eyes, who has a remarkable spirit and an abundance of energy. A month after the Challenger disaster, she travelled to twenty states, some two or more times, and she made over seventy public appearances all within a five month period. She is described as an inspirational, articulate, speaker who has a knack for handling the tough questions that come to her about the Challenger flight. She is so much in demand as a speaker that many of the requests she receives must be turned down or transferred to the other eight finalists who are stationed at different NASA Centers throughout the U.S. She still travels extensively for Teacher in Space and is gone for at least one week out of the month. The McCall School District and NASA divide her salary.

On April 8, 1986 she spoke at UI during Silver and Gold Days, was made an honorary alumna, and planted a tree on campus dedicated to the seven astronauts who died in the Challenger explosion. She expressed her feelings about Idaho in the article in Central Idaho as follows:

> I've had some wonderful experiences travelling around the country. I've met a lot of very good, nice people and I've been to some impressive places, but there's no place like Idaho. It's home. I'm glad I live here. I believe being from Idaho has helped me. I think I have a good perspective on life and part of that comes from living right here, in the mountains of McCall, Idaho.

MORRISON, Harry Winford   **1885-1971**   **Boise**

Often called the world's biggest builder, Morrison-Knudsen (M-K) Co. Inc., was started on a handshake, $600 cash and a few dozen tools. Among other projects, M-K built Hoover, Parker and Grand Coulee Dams.

One of the partners, Harry W. Morrison, was born February 23, 1885 in Turnbridge, DeWitt Co., Illinois. He attended local elementary and high schools there and then went to business college in Dixon, Ill. In 1904 he went to work for a Chicago company, Bates and Rogers Construction, as a time-keeper on the Minidoka Dam and Powerhouse project in Idaho. Next he went to work for the Minidoka project office of the U.S. Reclamation Service and worked successively as axman, rodman, chainman, levelman, foreman, draftsman and superintendent. In 1912 he met Morris H. Knudsen, an employee of the Reclamation Service, and an older expert in horseteam and earth-moving operations. They formed a partnership, on a hand-shake, March 1, 1912, which was to become the Morrison-Knudsen Co., Inc., a giant in the engineering construction business. At the time, Morrison was 27 and Knudsen 50. Their initial assets included $600 in cash, a dozen wheelbarrows, three dozen shovels, one dozen picks and a few other assorted tools.

Their first office was one room in a downtown Boise building. Their first job was a $14,000 subcontract to build a pumping station near Grand View, then linked to Mountain Home only by a dusty trail. Concrete had to be hauled up the hill with one man pushing the wheelbarrow and the other pulling it. But, when the job was finished there was a profit of $1,400 and the Morrison-Knudsen Co. was on its way. M-K now operates all over the world and has built many dams, air bases, power plants, seaports, irrigation systems, skyscrapers, drilled oil wells, mined coal -- you name it. They even contracted for asbestos removal in the UI Library basement remodel project. In Idaho M-K built the Lucky Peak, Anderson Ranch, Cabinet Gorge, Hell's Canyon, Brownlee Oxborn, Strike, Bliss and other dams.

Boise has always been M-K's headquarters and the Morrison family gave Boise the Ann Morrison Park. Harry Morrison was vice president and general manager of M-K until 1940 when he became president and general manager. In 1947 he became president and in 1960 chairman of the board. In 1950 he received an honorary doctorate from the UI.

Harry Morrison died July 19, 1971 and is buried in Morris Hill Cemetery in Boise.

O'CONNOR, John W. (Jack)   1902-78   Lewiston

The recognized authority on North American big game and sporting firearms lived in Lewiston. Author, editor, world-traveler, and big game hunter Jack O'Connor was born January 22, 1902 in Nogales, Arizona. He attended Arizona State Teachers College, 1921-23, the University of Arizona, 1923-24, received his B.A. from the University of Arkansas in 1925 and his M.A. from the University of Missouri in 1927.

His biographical sketch in <u>Who's Who Among PNW Writers</u> (1970) states:

> He has been a reporter and correspondent for several southern and mid-western newspapers; an associate professor of English at Arizona State Teachers College; professor of journalism at the University of Arizona; and shooting editor of <u>Outdoor Life Magazine</u> since 1941. O'Connor, an extensive world-wide traveler, is recognized as an authority on North American big game and sporting firearms. His articles are numerous and appear in such publications as <u>Field and Stream</u>, <u>Sports Afield</u>, <u>Esquire</u>, <u>Outdoor Life</u> etc. He has written two novels and a number of books on hunting and firearms. <u>Horse and Buggy West</u> (1969) is his autobiography. He lives at 725 Prospect Ave., Lewiston, Idaho.

Among his books are:

Conquest (1930)	Complete Book of Rifles and Shotguns (1961)
Boom Town (1938)	The Big Game of North America (1961)
Game in the Desert (1939)	Jack O'Connor's Big Game Hunts (1963)
Hunting in the Southwest (1945)	The Shotgun Book (1965)
Your Sporting Gun (1946)	Complete Book of Shooting (1965)
Hunting in the Rockies (1947)	Art of Hunting Big Game (1967)
The Rifle Book (1949)	Horse and Buggy West (1969)
The Big Game Rifle (1952)	
Arms and Ammunition (1952)	

Jack O'Connor left his big game trophies, an extensive collection, to UI where it is on display in the Life Sciences Building. He died January 20, 1978.

OLIVER, Dennis Dean   1929-   Boise

The World Almanac's Pro Rodeo Cowboy All Around Champions lists for the years 1963-65: "Dean Oliver, Boise, Idaho." Oliver was born in Kansas and moved with his family to Nampa when he was in high school. When his father died Oliver quit school in the 10th grade and worked on a farm near Boise to help feed the family. Dennis Dean Oliver never saw a big-time rodeo until he was 18, in 1948, when he and his brother Dale hitched a ride from their home in Boise to the Snake River Stampede in Nampa.

Rodeos then offered five different man-against-beast contests: bull-dogging (racing and wrestling steer to the ground), bull riding, saddle and bareback bronc riding (stay on-em as-long-as-long-as-you-can-events), and calf-roping. Championships were awarded in each division based on prize money accumulated during a season and "all around" championships were based on prize money won in two or more events. Oliver began entering rodeos in 1951, the start of a twenty-year career. His forte was calf-roping which requires an artful split-second co-ordination of rider, horse and lariat. He was world champion eight times. Oliver also did some bull-dogging. In 1960 he won the calf-roping championship by winning a record $28,841 for that single event in sixty rodeos. In 1961 at age 32 he was third in "all around." A five page spread in the Saturday Evening Post for December 2, 1961, with a full-page photo of the 6 foot 3 inch, 200 pound Boise cowboy, explained his expertise in the calf-roping event:

> The capacity crowd at Dallas Coliseum suddenly grew silent. Just off the arena floor a tall cowboy sat astride a sorrel in an open-faced stall. Beside him, in a closed chute, a 300-pound calf squirmed and stamped at the ground. The cowboy nodded and an attendant jerked open the chute door. The calf bolted into the arena. Then the horse cleared the stall, and the looped end of a twenty-five foot Manila rope hummed in the air over the cowboy's head. When the rope horse pulled up to within ten feet of the ducking, twisting calf, the cowboy sent his loop winging with the motion of a fast-ball pitcher, dropping it snugly over the calf's neck. The rope tightened, and the calf was jerked to an unceremonious stop.
> With effortless speed the cowboy leaped from his horse, picked up his calf, and flopped it on its side. From between his teeth he whipped a small looped "pigging" string and slipped it neatly over a foreleg. In an unbelievable blur of motion he crowded the calf's hind legs forward and tied them. Palms down, his hands shot out from the tie, signifying "time" for the rodeo officials. The cowboy was champion calf-roper Dean Oliver. His time in the tenth "go-round" of the National Finals Rodeo last January was a pulse-quickening 11.8 seconds.

Oliver went on to win the "all around" championships in 1963, 1964, and 1965.

POUND, Ezra   **1885-1972**   **Hailey**

One of the most important, and most controversial, literary figures of the Twentieth Century was poet Ezra Loomis Pound of Hailey. He was born October 20, 1885 in Hailey and raised by Presbyterian parents in Wyncote, a suburb of Philadelphia. He authored some ninety books and over 1500 articles. After receiving his Ph.D from Hamilton College in New York in 1905 and his M.A. from the University of Pennsylvania in 1906, Pound left the U.S. to live in Italy and London.

Academic American Encyclopedia says of Pound:

> Ezra Pound, whose poetry, criticism, and editorial work had a profound impact upon William Butler Yeats, and T.S. Eliot, left the U.S. in 1908 and became a central figure in the European literary avant-garde. Pound's imagist writings did much to introduce a strain of terse but evocative symbolism into modern literature.
> ... Pound quickly became preeminent as a modern writer and critic. He contributed to the London weekly New Age; and was literary advisor of the London magazine, the Egoist; and London correspondent of Harriet Monroe's magazine Poetry and the Little Review.
> Between 1914 and 1917, Pound launched both James Joyce and T.S. Eliot upon their literary careers, finding publishers for them and organizing financial assistance.

Pound left London and spent the years 1920-24 in Paris where he helped T.S. Eliot and Ernest Hemingway with their writing. From 1925-45 he lived in Rapallo, Italy and made over 300 radio broadcasts in support of Italian dictator Benito Mussolini over Rome Radio. He was indicted for treason by the U.S., arrested and placed in a prison camp in Pisa. He continued his writing in prison and was returned to the U.S. in 1945 but pronounced unfit for trial by reason of insanity and spent twelve years in St. Elizabeth's Hospital in Washington, D.C. Pound was released in 1958 and returned to Italy.

His major work, a modern epic poem called The Cantos, was something he worked on from 1915. While in prison in Pisa he produced a new segment, the Pisan Cantos (1948) which was considered superior to the rest. Pound died in Venice on November 1, 1972. The UI Library has a special collection of books by and about Ezra Pound. In 1978, UI awarded his daughter, Princess Mary de Rachewiltz, an honorary degree.

REINHARDT, Aurelia Henry   **1877-1948**   **Moscow/Lewiston**

The Toastmaster rose to introduce an honored guest. 'There are two things one should see on a trip to the West, he declared, "the Grand Canyon and Dr. Reinhardt." That was not the only compliment paid to Dr. Aurelia Henry Reinhardt in Boston last week. She was also elected moderator at the General Conference of the U.S. Unitarians, to succeed famed penologist Sanford Bates. At 63, Dr. Reinhardt thus became the first woman moderator of a large U.S. church. -- Time, June 3, 1940. Nationally noted (considered one of the ten most prominent women in the U.S.), educator, scholar, administrator Aurelia Henry Reinhardt was an instructor in English at UI from 1898-1901 and also taught English at Lewiston State Normal School, 1903-09.

Born April 1, 1877 in San Francisco, Henry obtained a B.L. from the University of California in 1898 and her Ph.D from Yale in 1905. Following a stint teaching at UI she studied at Yale on a scholarship, 1901-02, and on a fellowship, 1902-03. She was one of the first women graduate students at Yale. Henry resigned her teaching position in 1909 at Lewiston to marry Dr. George Frederick Reinhardt. When he died in 1914 she returned to teaching (1914-16) at the University of California. She then was chosen President of Mills College and served in that capacity from 1916-43. Mills College in Oakland, California is the second oldest women's college in the nation and was founded in 1852 for the daughters of the newly rich gold miners of California who did not want to send their daughters east for an education.

Henry was written up in both Time and Newsweek in 1940. The Time article described her as follows: "At 63, tall, big-boned, deep-voiced ... level-headed, unassuming, tireless." She wrote a number of articles for scholarly journals; edited, translated or contributed to several books, and had a considerable reputation as a scholar. She served on numerous boards and committees, and was president of the American Association of University Women from 1923-27.

Rafe Gibbs in Beacon for Mountain and Plain recalls that Miss Aurelia Henry, Associate Professor of Oratory, in 1898, produced two plays -- She Stoops To Conquer and The Rivals -- at UI which "played to packed houses in several towns on the way to and from Boise." "Among the members of the casts were Miss Henry, Burton L. French, who later became a Congressman from Idaho; William E. Lee, who later became a member of the U.S. Interstate Commerce Commission; and Homer David, who became a prominent Moscow businessman." Dr. Reinhardt returned to Moscow for a visit in 1947. She died January 28, 1948, age 70, in Oakland, California.

RENFREW, Malcolm Mackenzie   1910-   Moscow

We are all thankful for the invention of that material on pots and pans that prevents sticking -- Teflon.

Malcolm Renfrew, UI alum and professor emeritus of chemistry, was a member of the research team that invented Teflon, at Dupont, in 1938. Teflon is a trade name for a white, soft, waxy, and non-adhesive polymer of tetrafluoroethylene with a useful temperature range exceeding 500 degrees Fahrenheit. It has many uses including preventing food from sticking to cooking utensils.

Renfrew was born October 12, 1910 in Spokane and raised in Potlatch. He received his B.S. in chemistry from UI in 1932 and his M.S. (1934) and Ph.D (1938) from the University of Minnesota.

He worked as a research chemist in the plastics department at DuPont from 1938-44, supervisor of process development, 1944-46, and supervisor of product development, 1946-49. Next he worked at General Mills from 1949-54 where he was director of chemical research. From there he went to Spencer Kellogg and Sons where he was director of research and development from 1954-58.

In 1958 Renfrew returned to his alma mater as Head of the Physical Sciences Department, and served in that capacity from 1959-73. Knowing full well the value of research and getting started early in life, he established at UI in the summer of 1961 a program of research for undergraduate students. A total of ten young scientists worked on the first projects, which ranged from the study of movements of the air flow, a phenomenon to be dealt with in space flight, to work on the physical structure of new plastics.

Besides Teflon, Renfrew helped develop a plastic base for paint used on Navy ships to protect them against the effects of salt water. He has been a contributor to technical and trade magazines in the areas of plastics, coatings, safety, and chemical education and the recipient of numerous awards including:

>   Honorary Doctor of Science degree, UI - 1976
>   Excellence in Teaching Award from the Chemical Manufacturers Association - 1977
>   Outstanding Achievement Award, University of Minnesota - 1977
>   Elected to UI Hall of Fame - 1977
>   Chemical Health and Safety Award - 1985
>   Mosher Award - 1986

The UI Physical Sciences building is named for Malcolm Renfrew. He and his wife Carol still reside in Moscow.

REVERE, Paul　　　　　　**1942-**　　　　　　**Boise**

"One of the main products of Idaho has been Paul Revere. Not the Revolutionary War hero -- though that person's name and the style of dress of those days provide important bits of showmanship for the present-day namesake -- but the teen-age rock idol. Among many young people, the modern Paul Revere has become at least as well known as the original. He surely became much wealthier."
Encyclopedia of Pop, Rock and Soul, 1974.

Paul Revere was born Revere Dick in Boise in 1942 and became a teenage rock idol in the 1960s and 1970s with his group -- The Raiders. Revere worked as a barber in his teens and later became owner of a drive-in restaurant in Boise. He had learned to play piano and organ and supplemented his income by leading a small pop group at local clubs.

In the early 1960s an important addition to the band came in the form of a delivery boy. Mark Lindsay, of Cambridge, met Paul Revere while delivering bread to the drive-in restaurant. Revere told Lindsay he could join the band if he would learn to play an instrument. Mark went home and learned the saxophone.

In the early spring of 1963, Paul, Mark Lindsay, and disk jockey (later manager) Roger Hart pooled their savings of $57 and rented a small recording studio in Portland. They cut the single record that was to serve as the launching pad to stardom. That record was "Louie Louie."

It was at this time that Paul coined the name "Paul Revere and the Raiders." Revere and the Raiders (Mark Lindsay, Mike Smith, Phil Volk, and Jim "Harpo" Valley), had to brave, endure and outlast the onslaught of British (e.g., The Beatles) as well as a stateside group invasion of the pop music field, and in doing so broke all kinds of recording records.

During 1964 the group became one of the hottest attractions in the Pacific Northwest. In 1965 Mark Lindsay, who composed many of the band's songs, returned after an absence of about a year and the reorganized group made their first hit single, "Stepping Out." They came to the attention of Dick Clark and soon became regulars on his television show.

The Encyclopedia of Pop, Rock and Soul adds:
> Within a short time, the performers' dynamic rock beat and their Revolutionary-style outfits--complete with high boots, lace cuffs, frilled shirt fronts and George Washington-type hairdos--entered the consciousness of most of the nation's teenagers. The Raiders began to hit the single and LP charts regularly, a pattern that continued through most of the decade and into the 1970s.

REYNOLDS, Marjorie   1921-   Buhl

Marjorie Reynolds got her big break in movies when she starred with Bing Crosby and Fred Astaire in Irving Berlin's "Holiday Inn."

Marjorie was born Marjorie Goodspeed, August 21, 1921 in Buhl. Her name was changed to Marjorie Moore for movies and to Reynolds when she married Jack Reynolds of Samuel Goldwin studio. Her father was a physician and her mother an aspiring actress. When the family moved to Los Angeles, Marjorie's mother took her out to M-G-M and, at age three, she received a part in Revelation, a silent picture, for which she received $10. Mother and child got up a 3:00 a.m. to get out to Universal pictures in time to apply for work. They kept it up until the truant officer caught up with her.

Colliers for November 7, 1942 ran a three-page story on Marjorie in connection with the "Holiday Inn" movie:

> Miss Reynolds belongs to that line of Hollywood child wonders who receive each new blow with an expression of ecstasy. One might imagine that an actress who had spent twenty years in the profession and never reached a point farther north than leading lady in horse op'rys would be curdled by disappointment. Not at all. Miss Reynolds went gaily along, happy, ambitious and avowing that everybody in the business was wonderful. The leap from oblivion to being leading woman for Bing Crosby and Fred Astaire in a picture by Irving Berlin seemed merely a bit of poetic justice.

> When Mark Sandrich at Paramount began casting "Holiday Inn," he found all available candidates (for the part of Linda Mason) either experiencing motherhood (Mary Martin) or trussed up with constabulary writs (Ginger Rogers and Rita Hayworth).

In the movie, she sang a duet with Bing ("White Christmas") and he sang a song to her ("Easter Parade"). And she danced with Fred Astaire. The hotel chain took their name from this movie.

Marjorie went on to star in other pictures in the 1940s as a leading lady, including "Ministry of Fear," "Meet Me on Broadway," and "The Time of Their Lives." Then she went on to star in the successful television series, "The Life of Riley."

HAL
PHYFE

ROBB, Inez (Callaway)   1901(?)-79   Caldwell

Raised in Caldwell, Inez Robb was a nationally syndicated newspaper columnist and appeared in over 160 newspapers in the U.S. and abroad. She was born November 29, 1901(?) in Middletown, California on a 15,000 acre cattle ranch owned by her maternal grandfather. Her father was in the fruit-packing business and her childhood was spent in Caldwell.

Current Biography (1958) says of her:

> Inez Calloway started her newspaper career while a (Boise) high school student when,
> hearing that a Boise newspaper needed a high school reporter, she applied for
> the job and got it. She won a $200 College Women's Club scholarship to the
> University of Idaho and studied there for two years. After working for a
> year, she entered the University of Missouri and received her A.B. degree from
> its school of Journalism in 1924. Following graduation, she became general
> assignment reporter on the Tulsa, Oklahoma Daily World at $40 a week.

From there she went to the Chicago Tribune and then worked for the N.Y. Daily News from 1928-38. Robb joined the staff of INS (International News Service) in 1938 and for the next 15 years her column "Assignment: America" appeared daily in Hearst newspapers throughout America, as she travelled in over 40 countries. While with the Daily News she covered the coronation of King George VI in London and the wedding of the Duke and Duchess of Windsor. When Pan American Airlines inaugurated its European service and made the first round-trip flight across the Atlantic in 1939, Inez Robb was on the plane, according to Current Biography.

She won the Holmes Award in 1948 and the New York Newspaper Women's Club in 1957 "for the best column in any field." UI awarded her an honorary Doctor of Literature degree in 1959. She visited Boise often and once wrote:

> Boise is one of the most beautiful towns in America, a gem nestled at the towering
> foothills of the Sawtooths. The Boise River flows through the city like the Seine
> through Paris, its banks a continuous park.
> An outpost, huh? We got an art museum, a historical museum, and handsomest
> railroad depot in the U.S.A., one of the biggest airports and a junior college that
> imports football players just as any Eastern school.

Current Biography says her writing "was noted for lively, provocative style and content and was honored for reporting by many news organizations." Inez Robb died April 4, 1979 in Tucson, Arizona.

ROBERTSON, Frank Chester   1890-1969   Moscow

One of the nation's most prolific authors (over 200 books and 2,000 articles), Frank Robertson was born January 12, 1890, just outside of Moscow. Many of his western stories were based on his own experiences as a child in northern Idaho. The Robertsons were poor, lived in several places in Latah County, and never able to get out of debt. In 1901 the family moved to Chesterfield (Bannock County) and Frank Robertson lived there until 1924 when he became a migratory ranch hand.
Who's Who Among PNW Authors says of him:

> His only formal schooling was received in the Chesterfield Grade School, and after graduation he was a migratory ranch hand for several years. In 1914 Robertson homesteaded a dry farm on the Chesterfield east bench. On July 11, 1919 he married Winnie Bowman, and to them were born three children. He went broke in 1921, began writing in that year, and moved to Utah in 1924.
> Robertson sold his first story, a novel, The Hole in the Rock, to Adventure Magazine in 1921. In addition to his scores of Western novels published in the U.S., he has published more than one hundred novels in the British Empire. He is one of thirty-nine authors included in the famous Century Omnibus series (London) in a volume entitled A Century of Western Stories. Robertson has also published several hundred stories in the U.S. and in England. Several novels have been syndicated in newspapers and several have been made into pictures. In 1954, Robertson was presented a silver spur by the Western writers of America for best juvenile book of the year, Sagebrush Sorrel. Ram in the Thicket (1950), his autobiography, recounts his life in northern Idaho.

An article in the Daily Idahonian for July 4, 1987 compared Robertson and Carol Brink:

> Two Moscow Authors Went Different Directions
> Frank Chester Robertson and Carol Ryrie Brink grew up at about the same time. They both became prolific authors of books for children and adults. That is where the similarity ends.
> ... Robertson left no such legacy in the town, and indeed few people have heard of him or know of his Moscow roots. During his life he was one of the nation's most prolific western novelists.
> While not an instant success, he nevertheless began to produce a steady stream of pulp articles and western novels, many of which were translated into different languages, and almost all of which were more popular in Europe than in the U.S.

Frank Chester Robertson died in Springfield, Utah in 1969.

ROBINSON, Frank Bruce   **1885-1948**   **Moscow**

Excerpts from the Idahonian for July 4, 1987, recall Frank Robinson and Psychiana:

ROBINSON'S MAIL-ORDER RELIGION PUT MOSCOW ON MAP
In the 1930s a prominent sign stood at the entrance to the city and it
read:

> Moscow, Idaho
> Known the World Over
> as the Home of Psychiana
> The New Psychological Religion

This heralded one of the most controversial issues and one of the most
controversial persons to appear in Moscow during the century of the city's existence.
The issue was Psychiana, "the power that will bring new life to a spiritually
dead world," and the person was Dr. Frank B. Robinson, its founder.

Born of British parents in New York City July 5, 1885, Robertson grew up in England. At 15, he and his
brother Sydney came to Belleville, Ontario, Canada. He was a self-educated pharmacist and practiced
in Oregon, California, Washington and Idaho. Robinson came to Moscow in April, 1928 and was
employed as a pharmacist at the Corner Drug. With his evenings free, he could devote himself to his
religious vision of the future. He started Psychiana in 1929 and it soon became the largest private
employer in Moscow and was responsible for Moscow obtaining first class status as a post office.
Psychiana flourished for over twenty years and was reputed to be the world's largest mail-order religion.
At peak advertising times, Psychiana sent out as many as 50,000 pieces of mail in a single day. There
were subscribers in 67 countries.

The Idahonian article explained the organization's growth and citizen feelings about its founder as
follows:

> Psychiana grew essentially out of the Great Depression when times were hard and
> work was scarce. People were discouraged and Psychiana provided a hope.
> But throughout the community the feeling persisted that Robinson was only into
> religion as a business to make money and that Psychiana basically was a scam.
> But most people in Moscow didn't know much about it, think much about it, and chose
> to ignore it.

Robinson made enemies however, and there were charges that led to a deportation trial in 1936. He was
indicted on charges of falsifying his passport and claiming to be an American citizen. Senator Borah
intervened and the deportation order was modified. Robinson became a naturalized citizen in 1942.
That year he suffered the first of a series of heart attacks that eventually killed him October 19, 1948. The
Psychiana papers are maintained in the UI Library Special Collections Department.

ROMNEY, George   **1907–**   **Oakley**

Back in 1914, which was a bad year for potato prices, a farm family near Oakley
did more than its share in trying to get rid of the surplus of potatoes by
eating them three times a day. A seven-year-old boy in the family said that
he ate so many potatoes that he "felt like a sack of them." His name was
George Romney. Later he became the President of American Motors Corporation,
Governor of Michigan, U.S. Secretary of Housing and Urban Development, and a front-
runner for the 1968 Republican presidential nomination. -- Rafe Gibbs, Beckoning The Bold.

George Romney was born on July 8, 1907 in Chihuahua, Mexico. When Romney was five, Pancho Villa
expelled American families from Mexico. The family moved to Los Angeles and then Idaho, to Oakley,
south of Burley. The senior Romney was in the contracting business and was to suffer a series of
financial reverses. These experiences in overcoming difficulties influenced George Romney's life and
business career.
According to Current Biography (1958):
Romney took his first job at the age of eleven as a sugar harvester. Later he became
a skilled lath-and-plaster workman. From 1922-26 he worked his way through
Latter-Day Saints University in Salt Lake City, Utah. He then served two years in
England and Scotland as a Mormon missionary, an experience he believes sharpened his
abilities at debate, quick thinking, and persuasion. After a brief period of
study at the University of Utah in 1929 he went to Washington, D.C.
Romney worked for a year as a typist for Senator David I. Walsh of Massachusetts and attended George
Washington University. In 1930 he became an apprentice for Alcoa and was sent to Los Angeles as a
salesman. From 1932-38 he worked in Washington, D.C. as a lobbyist for Alcoa and the Aluminum
Wares Association. He was President of the Washington Trade Association Executives from 1938-39.

Romney attracted the attention of men in the auto industry and he served in various capacities for the
Automobile Manufacturers Association from 1939-54 when he became President of American Motors.
He felt the only way an independent company could compete with the "big three" was to make a car they
didn't have and thus came about the "compact car" in American life -- the Rambler. By the end of 1957
the company stopped producing their big cars -- Nash and Hudson -- and concentrated on the Rambler,
and moved from thirteenth to seventh in car production standings. Romney served as Governor of
Michigan from 1963-69 and was appointed by President Nixon as Secretary of Housing and Urban
Development, serving from 1969-73. No small potatoes for a boy from Idaho.

SACAJAWEA   ca.1790-1812   **Salmon/Lemhi**
                 or 1884   **Valley**

The best known of the Shoshoni Indians was Sacajawea who served as interpreter and guide for Lewis and Clark on their long journey from St. Louis to the Pacific Ocean in 1804-05. She was born near Salmon in the Lemhi Valley ca. 1790 and thus would have been about 14 when she met Lewis and Clark. Readers Encyclopedia of The American West says of Sacajawea:

> Her father was a Shoshoni chieftain but in 1800, when about ten years of age, she
> was captured by a party of Hidatsa near the Three Forks of the Missouri River. Subse-
> quently she and another captive girl were purchased and taken to wife by Toussaint
> Charbonneau, a Canadian then living among the Hidatsa. The explorers Lewis and
> Clark found Charbonneau at Ft. Mandan in the winter of 1804-05 and engaged him
> as interpreter for their expedition, with the specific understanding that Sacajawea
> be allowed to accompany the party. Eight weeks before the expedition departed from
> Fort Mandan, she gave birth to her first child, a son named Jean Baptiste Charbonneau
> and called Pomp or Pompey by William Clark. This infant she carried on a cradleboard
> when the party headed upriver in early April, 1805.

Sacajawea proved to be more of an asset to the party than Charbonneau. She was familiar with Idaho, an area Lewis and Clark knew nothing about, knew the different dialects, and influenced Indians along the way that this party, with a woman and child, was friendly and not bent on war. When the Lewis and Clark party reached the Lemhi Valley, they were first met by a band a Shoshonis led by Chief Cameahwait who turned out to be Sacajawea's brother. They of course gave the party a warm welcome. The expedition successfully made it to the mouth of the Columbia River and then returned to the Mandan villages in 1806. From this point Sacajawea disappears from the pages of history. There are differing views on what happened to her next. One is that she accompanied her husband to St. Louis about 1809 and returned in 1811 to the West only to die of fever in 1812. The other is that she lived for some time among the Commanche and later returned to her own people on the Wind River Reservation, where she died in 1884.

> The academic controversy about Sacajawea's death date and place has not
> been resolved to the satisfaction of everyone. But this much can be
> said about her: she was a woman of unusual courage and the position she
> occupies in American history as the heroine of the Lewis and Clark
> expedition is deserved and secure. -- Crowder. Tales of Eastern Idaho.

SARETT, Lewis Hastings   **1917-**   **Viola**

Merck and Co. chemist, Lew Sarett, who lives in retirement in Viola, near Moscow, prepared the first synthetic cortisone in 1944, and is a member of the National Inventors Hall of Fame.

Born December 22, 1917 in Champaign, Illinois, Sarett received his B.S. from Northwestern University in 1939 and his Ph.D from Princeton in 1942. That year he joined Merck Research Laboratories in Rahway, New Jersey as a research chemist.

For his work, Sarett was inducted, in 1981, into the National Inventors Hall of Fame which was established in 1973 and dedicated to the individuals who conceived the great technological advances which this nation fosters through its patent system. Members include Thomas Edison, Alexander Graham Bell, Marconi, Eastman, Dow, Steinmetz, and Henry Ford, among others. Of the sixty-seven so far inducted, two have Idaho connections -- Farnsworth and Sarett.

The biographical sketch on Sarett in the <u>National Inventors Hall of Fame</u> publication says:

> Sarett prepared the first synthetic cortisone in 1944, when Merck &
> Co. was a participant in a government effort to improve military medicine,
> and four years later the Mayo Clinic demonstrated the efficacy of this
> hormone against rheumatoid arthritis.
>
> In 1949, he and several collaborators initiated an alternative
> synthesis commencing with raw materials derivable from coal, air,
> lime and water. This led to the first route which was independent of
> naturally occurring starting materials. For this work Sarett received
> the American Chemical Society Award for Creative Chemistry in 1964, one
> of his many honors and awards. He has collaborated on approximately
> 100 technical papers and patents.

Sarett's career at Merck & Co. spanned some forty years. He served as Senior Vice President for Science and Technology his last few years before he retired in 1982 and moved to Idaho.

SHIPMAN, Nell   **1892-1970**   **Priest Lake**

Silent screen writer, director and actress Nell Shipman produced films in the 1920s around Priest Lake. She was born Helen Foster Barnham, October 25, 1892 in Victoria, British Columbia. While playing the lead in the Rex Beach play "The Barrier" in 1910, she married the producer, Ernie Shipman. She fell down some hotel stairs in Fargo, on tour, and suffered a severely sprained ankle. Nell went to her brother's cabin on Lake Coeur d'Alene to recuperate, while "The Barrier" played in Spokane with a new leading lady.

Her son, Barry, was born in 1912. While working on a film at Lake Tahoe, with Barry working as a child actor, Nell became the director. The man directing the film ran off to marry the leading lady. For a time Shipman acted in films for Cecil B. DeMille. She appeared in a number of silent films including:

>   The Black Wolf   Back to God's Country
>   God's Country and the Woman   The Girl from God's Country
>   Grub Stake

Some of these were produced in north Idaho during the years 1923-26. Her autobiography, <u>The Silent Screen and My Talking Heart</u>, was published by Boise State University in 1987 and the cover blurb says:

>   Canadian-born Silent Film writer, director, and star Nell Shipman came to Idaho's
>   Priest Lake from Hollywood in 1922 with her young son, a doomed lover-producer,
>   a future Academy Award winning cinematographer, and a menagerie of bobcats,
>   bears, elk, eagles, deer, dogs -- over 70 animals transported by rail,
>   truck, car and barge to her eastern lakeside studio, Lionhead Lodge. There
>   Shipman sought authentic film locales and, in more urban territory, financing
>   angels. She found both -- along with murderous and sympathetic locals in
>   a harsh and beautiful land where greed and a changing film industry combined to
>   leave her bankrupt and rich in experience for an unforgettable memoir,
>   portions of which have appeared in <u>Atlantic Monthly</u>.
>
>   Shipman's candid saga chronicles the career of a girl who joined a travelling
>   theatrical company while still a teenager and who became a woman film pioneer,
>   a movie-maker who insisted on the humane treatment of animals, the value
>   of location shooting, and the necessity of independent production in film
>   making.

Although Shipman stopped producing films in the mid-twenties, she continued to write stories and screenplays. One, "Wings in the Dark" (1935), starred Myrna Loy and Cary Grant. She finished writing her autobiography in February of 1969 and died in 1970 at her home in Cabazon, California.

SHRONTZ, Frank Anderson   1931-   Boise

The Chief Executive Officer of Boeing, the nation's largest commercial aircraft manufacturer, was born in Boise and is a UI alum. Frank Anderson Shrontz was born December 14, 1931 in Boise. He received his LLB from UI in 1954 and his MBA from Harvard in 1958. He also did post graduate work at George Washington University and at Stanford. Joining Boeing in 1958, Shrontz held the following positions:

      Asst. Director, Contract Administration, 1958-65

      Asst. to the Vice President for Commercial Airplane Group, 1965-67

      Asst. Director, New Airplane Group, 1967-69

      Director, Commercial Sales Operations, 1970-73

From 1973-77 he was in Washington, D.C. as Assistant Secretary of the Air Force and with the Department of Defense. In 1976 he received the Distinguished Service Award from the U.S. Department of Defense. Upon returning to Boeing, he served as:

      Vice President for Planning and Contracts, 1977-78

      Vice President and General Manager, 707/727/737 Division, 1978-82, and

      Vice President for Sales and Marketing, 1982-84

In 1985 he became President and in 1986 CEO of Boeing. Shrontz lives on Mercer Island, in Seattle. In 1986 he was named to the UI Hall of Fame. Besides being the nation's largest commercial aircraft manufacturer, Boeing is also the 4th largest exporter and the 6th largest company in government contracts.

It may be worthy of note that Dean Dickson Thornton, current Boeing Commercial Airplane Company president, also has Idaho connections. Born January 5, 1929 in Yakima, Washington, Thornton graduated from Lewiston High School and received his B.S. in Business from UI in 1952. After serving in the Air Force as the first lieutenant, 1952-54, and as a CPA accountant for Touche, Ross & Co. in Seattle from 1954-63, he went to work for Boeing as treasurer, controller from 1963-70. He held various other positions with Boeing until becoming president in 1985. In 1986 he was elected to the UI Hall of Fame.

"Boeing had $19.9 billion in commercial jet orders in 1987 and industry analysts said Boeing could enjoy a fourth straight year of record orders, perhaps as high as $25 billion." -- <u>Idahonian</u>, May 27, 1988.

SIMPLOT, J.R. (Jack)   **1909-**   **Boise**

A 1987 newspaper poll indicated J.R. Simplot was the most powerful man in Idaho, after Governor Andrus. He remains on <u>Fortune</u> magazine's list of the world's wealthiest people. John Richard Simplot was born January 4, 1909 in Dubuque, Iowa. Two years later his family settled on a farm in Declo. Although a high school dropout Simplot saw the handwriting on the wall with respect to dehydrated and frozen foods.

<u>The History of Idaho</u> by Beal and Wells has a biographical sketch of Simplot which says in part:

> At the age of nineteen he began his career as a produce commission merchant at Burley. He quickly turned attention to the development of enterprises of his own, and by 1941 was the state's largest shipper of potatoes and onions. He had by then acquired thirty potato and onion packing warehouses and a number of farms, principally in the Burley area. Seeing a promising future in dehydrated foods, he began construction of a small onion dehydrator at Caldwell in 1941. Facilities were expanded after Pearl Harbor and this plant became the largest supplier of dehydrated potatoes to the armed forces. Between 1942 and 1945, Mr. Simplot produced more than thirty-three million pounds of dried potatoes annually for the government and won an Army-Navy "E."
>
> Canning and quick-freezing operations were added in 1946-47. Over twenty food products now (1970) come from the Caldwell (Food Processing Division) plant including "minute" potatoes, frozen french fries, frozen potato patties, frozen diced potatoes, onion flakes, onion powder, canned corn, fruit and vegetables, frozen corn, and other fruits and vegetables.

Simplot is credited with making the first commercial frozen french fries and now provides most of McDonald's fries. The company has expanded into many other endeavors and J.R. still runs his diversified business from a large office on the top of One Capitol Center, Boise. The plain spoken, unpretentious and patriotic Simplot can easily see from his office the 30 x 50 foot American flag that flies over his home in the Foothills.

The multi-millionaire philanthropist has donated over $10 million to the College of Idaho and serves as honorary co-chairman for the UI Centennial Campaign. He received an honorary Doctor of Administrative Science from UI in 1975.

Some quotes from Simplot:

> **On success** - I'm not smarter than anyone else...I knew how to get a penny from a potato and when I got that penny I saved it.
>
> **On Idaho** - I'm never going to leave Idaho...I've been everywhere, and there's no place better.

J.R. Simplot's license plates (1982) carry the words "Mr. Spud."

SMITH, E.E. (Doc)   **1890-1965**   **Moscow**

The "Dean of Science Fiction Writers" during the 1930s and 1940s, UI alum "Doc" Smith is credited with writing the forerunners of Star Trek and Star Wars movies. Born Edward Elmer Smith May 1, 1890 in Sheboygan, Wisconsin, he graduated with a B.S. in chemistry from UI in 1914. In 1919 he received his Ph.D. in food chemistry from George Washington University in Washington, D.C. Twentieth Century Science Fiction Writers in his biographical sketch says:

> Served in an explosives arsenal during World War II. Married Jeannie McDougall; one daughter and one son. Worked as ranch hand, lumber jack, silver miner, and surveyor, before becoming a chemist, specializing in food mixes. Manager of General Mix Division of J.W. Allen and Co., 1945; retired in the early 1960s. Recipient: First Fandom Hall of Fame Award, 1964. Guest of Honor, 2nd World Science Fiction Convention, 1940. Died 31 August 1965.

A listing of about twenty of his books follows, starting with the Skylark of Space and ending with Masters of Space (1976).

The MosCon V Science Fiction convention was held in his honor, September 1983 and Smith was inducted into the UI Hall of Fame in 1984. His first book, Skylark of Space was originally published in 1928 and has been in print ever since. A number of his main characters were modelled after fellow students at UI. According to the Gem of the Mountains, Doc had a lively college career at UI. He sang baritone in the Men's Glee Club and bass in Gilbert and Sullivan light operas. He played guitar in the Mandolin Club; was a member of the chemistry, rifle and chess clubs; was a first lieutenant in the Cadet Battalion; drew cartoons for the 1913 Gem and graduated with "A" honors. A few excerpts about Smith from Twentieth Century Science Fiction Writers follow:

> It is difficult if not impossible to overestimate the impact of E.E. "Doc" Smith in 20th century science fiction. He developed and perfected the space opera, a form which had existed only in a rudimentary state prior to his work.
> ... With the appearance of Smith's The Skylark of Space in Amazing Stories, in 1928, Smith achieved pre-eminence in the field and never was surpassed. Once Smith was established, numerous others wrote within the arena he created. More recently the film "Star Wars" has been classed by many viewers as the purest space opera yet produced in dramatic form. ...By these criteria Smith was the absolute champion of his realm.

SMITH, Paul J.   **1906-85**   **Caldwell**

The composer of numerous Walt Disney feature film and cartoon scores, Paul J. Smith was raised in Caldwell. Jerome Smith wrote about his brother in <u>Cold Drill Extra</u> (1984). Following are some excerpts:

>Paul Joseph Smith was born in Calumet, Michigan on October 30, 1906, the son of Anna M. and Joseph J. Smith, an accountant with Calumet and Hecla Mining Co., and a professional musician. Paul began his music study early there with excellent teachers in piano, violin and harmony. In 1919 his family moved to Caldwell where he continued study ... he graduated from Caldwell High School in 1923, then attended the College of Idaho for two years, playing violin in the school orchestra, and piano and banjo with dance bands.
>
>In the fall of 1925, Paul entered the Bush Conservatory, Chicago, studying and teaching piano and violin there. After two years at the Conservatory he enrolled at UCLA, where he graduated with a B.A. in 1928 after directing "The Spring Extravaganza" that year.
>
>Soon after graduation, Paul was employed by Walt Disney Productions, where he wrote and recorded the music for animated shorts numbering in the hundreds over the years.

He did the same for Disney's full-length features as well, including "Snow White," "Fantasia," and "Pinnochio" for which he won the Academy Award for Best Musical Score. Paul Smith also did the music composition and recording for the Disney Nature Series which included "The Living Desert," "Beaver Valley," etc., and the songs for the Mickey Mouse Club children's TV programs.

The musical score for "Pinnochio" is considered one of the finest Paul Smith ever wrote. It should be noted that in these animated films there must be music for a solid seventy-five minutes without a break. The musical score not only supplements the action but "plays a major role in creating the desired moods." Smith worked at the Disney studio from 1934-62 and had eight Oscar nominations.

In May, 1955, Smith was awarded an honorary Doctorate of Music from the College of Idaho. Smith retired from active writing in 1968 and lived in Burbank until his death of a cardiac arrest January 25, 1985, at the age of 78.

SORRELS, Rosalie (Stringfellow)   1933-   Boise

Rosalie Sorrels is an internationally acclaimed folksinger, song writer and storyteller. Her lasting contribution to the 1990 Idaho Centennial is a collection of Idaho Folk songs. Born Rosalie Stringfellow in Adams County in 1933, she grew up in small towns in Idaho and Utah and now lives near Boise. She has recorded over a dozen albums of her songs and has made thousands of concert appearances in the U.S. and abroad.

Some excerpts from an article about her in the <u>Encyclopedia of Folk, Country and Western Music</u> (1983) follow:

> A folk artist in the traditional sense, Rosalie Sorrels collected authentic
> stories and songs of the people and wrote material that satisfied her own
> creative needs, rather than bending to the tides of commercialism.
> Rosalie was aided in her efforts by husband Jim Sorrels, whom she married
> in 1950. Sorrels, who played guitar, enjoyed singing and playing music
> with Rosalie and also contributed new songs himself, some collected while
> he was working as a telephone lineman for Mountain States Telephone Company
> in Idaho. The Sorrels jointly went on folk song collecting expeditions
> in the 1950s and 1960s and at one point taught classes in folk guitar at
> the University of Utah.
>
> Sorrels' reputation as a folksinger began to reach folk adherents well
> beyond the U.S. mountain states and eventually led to her first recordings
> for Folkways Records. One of her first Folkways LPs was the 1961 "Folk
> Songs of Idaho and Utah." The album sparked interest in her work and led
> to increased concerts in folk clubs and on the college circuit.
>
> During the 1970s, the pattern was not much different from the previous
> decade. Sorrels gave folk music concerts in many parts of the U.S. and
> in other countries, but at a relatively leisurely pace, and recorded a
> new album every now and then.

Sorrels was the winner of the 1985 Idaho Governor's Award for Excellence. The songs she collected while travelling around Idaho are published in the Idaho Centennial Songbook.

Although she has traveled a lot and lived in Idaho and Utah, she spent summers, growing up, with her grandparents in Twin Falls. She now lives in Grimes, near Idaho City.

SPALDING, Rev. Henry Harmon   1803-74   Lapwai

A number of Idaho firsts belong to Rev. Henry Spalding, the Presbyterian missionary to the Indians who came to Lapwai in 1836. He and his wife set up Idaho's first school, they had the first white child born in Idaho, had the first printing press in Oregon Country and produced the first book printed in Idaho. The Reader's Encyclopedia of the American West says of Spalding:

> Oregon missionary and pioneer. Born out of wedlock in Wheeler, New York, to an uncaring mother, neglected by his foster father, and jilted by his sweetheart Narcissa Prentiss, who later married Marcus Whitman, Spalding was embittered before he entered upon missionary work in the Pacific Northwest in 1836. In that year he traveled to the Oregon Country with his wife, Eliza Hart, and the Whitmans and William Gray. Setting up his mission at Lapwai, near present-day Lewiston, Idaho, in the heart of the Nez Perce Country, Spalding began the arduous task of converting the Indians.

The Whitmans had stopped near present-day Walla Walla to establish their mission among the Cayuse Indians.

The Nez Perce were friendly to the Spaldings and brought them food and helped them build needed buildings. In return, Spalding treated the sick, taught the Indians to farm, started the first school, where Mrs. Spalding taught Indian pupils of all ages reading, writing and religion as well as various crafts such as spinning, weaving, sewing and knitting. Having no books, she printed her own, by hand.

Idaho's first white child, Eliza Spalding, named after her mother, was born November 15, 1837. Spalding started operating the first printing press in the Pacific Northwest on May 16, 1839 when the press was sent from Honolulu as a gift from a church there. The first book was a small eight-page children's book in the Nez Perce language. Books and pamphlets turned out on the press included a primer, hymnbook, code of law for the Nez Perce, and a translation of the Gospel by Matthew. Most were in Nez Perce.

After the Whitman Massacre in 1847, Spalding left Lapwai for the Willamette Valley where he became a farmer. While there he was made commissioner of schools and in 1851 served as Indian agent. He returned to Lapwai in 1862.

Some of the Spalding imprints are in the UI Library Special Collections Department and the Spalding papers include collections at Washington State University and Whitman College. Spalding died in 1874, age 71.

STEINMAN, David Barnard   **1886-1960**   **Moscow**

A UI professor who built his first bridge with the help of Boy Scouts became the world's greatest bridge-builder. In his lifetime David B. Steinman designed over four hundred bridges on five continents. Steinman was born June 11, 1886 in New York City's lower East Side in a three-room tenement, in the shadows of the Brooklyn Bridge. He showed an interest in bridges as a young boy. At 13 he became a student at the City College of New York and won a special pass allowing him to climb the steelwork and observe the engineers on the Williamsburg Bridge, then being built over the East River.
Current Biography (1957) says of Steinman:

> In 1906 he graduated summa cum laude, receiving his B.S. degree and three
> scholarships worth $650. In addition he was awarded twelve medals
> and prizes and was elected to Phi Beta Kappa. In 1909 he earned both the C.E.
> and M.A. degrees from Columbia. His engineering thesis was entitled "The Design
> of the Henry Hudson Memorial Bridge as a Steel Arch." At the age of twenty-four
> he joined the faculty of the University of Idaho in Moscow. He taught there
> from 1910 to 1914 when he became full professor. In 1911 he received the Ph.D.
> degree from Columbia. His doctoral dissertation was published as a book by
> Van Nostrand and became a best seller among technical publications.

He wrote over 700 publications, some fifteen books including volumes of poetry. At UI he went from instructor to full professor in four years, reportedly being the youngest full professor in the U.S. When he first applied for the position he thought it was in Iowa. When he arrived in Moscow, he bought a horse named "Bill" and was soon a familiar figure riding from town to campus. He was known as "the professor on the white horse." Steinman covered the mile and one-half in five minutes, faster than most make it in their cars. Once he was arrested for speeding. There was an ordinance "declaring it a misdemeanor to ride a horse faster than eight miles an hour on the city streets." When the magistrate asked the officer if he would swear the professor was going over eight miles an hour, the officer replied, "Yes, your honor, I will swear he was going over twenty-eight miles an hour." He was assessed a $3 fine. In 1910 Steinman started the first Boy Scout troop in Idaho. His first bridge was built by those scouts, at "Camp Half-a-hat," across the Potlatch River. It was a cantilever bridge, made of logs, spanning forty feet. He drew the plans for the largest bridge in South America, the longest cantilever bridge in the U.S., the longest suspension bridge in the world, the Messina Strait Bridge in Italy, the Liberty Bridge in N.Y.C. and the Mackinac Straits Bridge, which opened in 1957, cost $100 million, was second in length only to the Golden Gate, and connected northern and southern Michigan.

Steinman died August 21, 1960 in New York at the age of 74.

TRUEBLOOD, Cecil Whittaker (Ted)   1913-82   Boise/Wilder

Called "The Dean of Outdoor Writers," Ted Trueblood was born June 26, 1913 in Boise and grew up on his parents' farm near Wilder. He attended Wilder High, and the College of Idaho for three years. Trueblood worked as a reporter, was an avid conservationist, and an outdoor writer read by millions.

A biographical sketch on him in Who's Who Among PNW Writers (1970) said:
> A Writer and outdoorsman, he has also had experience as a reporter on the defunct Boise Capitol News, the Deseret News (Salt Lake City) and the News and Observer (Raleigh, N.C.). He has written regularly and prolifically for many sportsmen's magazines, has been outdoor editor or gun editor of several, and has been advisor on sporting books to T. Y. Crowell and Company. He has been fishing editor of Field and Stream. He writes regularly for True and other men's outdoor magazines.

At that time he had published seven books including: The Angler's Handbook (1949), Fishing Handbook (1951), Ted Trueblood on Hunting (1953), The Hunter's Handbook (1954), How to Catch More Fish (1955) On Hunting (1955) and Camping Handbook (1955). His last was The Ted Trueblood Hunting Treasury (1978).

His first article on the outdoors was written as a senior at Wilder High. He went to New York City in the early 1930s to write for Field and Stream and returned to Idaho in the late 1930s after witnessing a recently retired neighbor die of a heart attack. That prompted him to quit his job and return to the West "determined to hunt, fish and write about it." In a chapter from a book he asked "Why work hard and save money and then die before I had a chance to enjoy the things for which I had been saving?" He wrote for some forty years.

Trueblood died Sunday, September 12, 1982 at his home in Nampa, of an apparent self-inflicted gunshot wound at the age of 69. He had been suffering from cancer for several years and had undergone surgery and chemotherapy. A Boise Statesman editorial (September 15, 1982) concluded by saying: "His sentences were simple, lucid statements spun in magic. Sportsmen said Trueblood's articles put them in the places of which he wrote, and it was true."
Trueblood said:
> (He found pleasure) in the simple things my ancestors did many centuries ago, such as camping out and cooking dinner over a wood fire. Then I like to sit beside it and watch the twinkling stars emerge and listen to the wavering call of a coyote while the clean, sweet smoke rises, like the wraith of some long-gone hunter, to vanish in the darkening sky.
> - The Idaho Statesman, September 14, 1982.

TURNER, Lana   **1921–**   **Wallace**

Undoubtedly Idaho's best known actress is Lana Turner. Current Biography (1943) wrote early in her movie career:

> Known as America's "Sweater Girl," Lana Turner has securely established herself as one of the most popular actresses of the modern screen. She has been voted the sweetheart of Sigma Phi, Phi Delta Theta, and countless other fraternities. She has had the offer of half an island if she would move in.
>
> . . . A combination of Danish, Swedish, Irish, French, English, and Spanish stock, America's Sweater Girl was born on February 8, 1920 (it was actually 1921) in Wallace, Idaho where her father, Virgil Turner, worked as a foreman in the mines. Her real name is Julia Jean Mildred Frances Turner and her friends in school used to call her "Judy." When three years old she made her theatrical debut -- if one may call it that -- at a charity fashion show where her mother was one of the models. Before anyone could stop her she rushed upon the stage and did an impromptu dance in front of the audience.
>
> Soon (when she was six) the family moved to San Francisco where tragedy awaited them. One winter night Virgil was "blackjacked" by some thugs and after that Mrs. Turner had to support herself and her seven-year old daughter by working in a beauty parlor. Lana at the time went to the Convent of the Immaculate Conception and her great ambition in life was to become a nun.

She changed her mind when she learned nuns had to cut their hair. Instead she became a junior high school cheerleader and was decisively re-elected, "an early triumph of mass judgement." Moving to Los Angeles for her mother's health, Lana entered Hollywood High -- and her film career began. She was "discovered" in the drugstore across the street from school and eventually introduced to director Mervin LeRoy. She was 15. LeRoy didn't like any of her given names so she suggested "Lana." Why? "It just came to her." It would be rare today for someone to get into the movies without so much as a day's experience acting but she did just that.

Her first picture, "They Won't Forget," (1937) was followed by a host of others such as "The Adventures of Marco Polo," "Love Finds Andy Hardy," "Calling Dr. Kildare," "Ziegfield Girl," "The Postman Always Rings Twice," "Madame X," and "Peyton Place." For "Peyton Place" Lana received an Academy Award nomination for Best Actress. She made two, three, sometimes four films a year during the 1940s, 1950s, and 1960s. She appeared opposite all the leading men during those years and more recently has had a number of television roles including "Falcon Crest." It took her years of hard work to overcome the Sweater Girl image. Though born in Wallace she lived as a child in Burke and never returned except for a war bond drive in 1942. Her autobiography, Lana - the Lady, the Legend, the Truth was published by Dutton in 1982.

PHOTO: Mrs. J.B. Turner and Lana (1924)

VOIGTLANDER, Ted W.   **1913-**   **Kellogg**

This Hollywood cinematographer from Kellogg won fourteen Emmy nominations, three Emmys, six Eastman Kodak awards, and was named Cinematographer of the Year in 1974. Voigtlander was born in Kellogg, August 3, 1913 and attended public school and Union High there. He studied at UI from 1931-34 and transferred to the University of Washington where he received his B.S. in 1936.

In a 1983 letter containing a biographical sketch of himself, Voigtlander wrote:

> I travelled to Los Angeles in 1937 and went to work at M.G.M. studios as a typist and office boy. After a short while I became assistant to Lazlo Willinger, a world-famous portrait photographer, in his studio at M.G.M. I was transferred to the camera department to work as an equipment clerk. In 1943 I became an assistant motion picture cameraman, working my way up from assistant to camera operator, becoming Director of Photography in 1960. During that "growing up" time, I travelled the world for M.G.M. studios, and was involved in the production of many foreign motion pictures such as:

King Solomon's Mines	(filmed in)	East Africa
Kim		India
Valley of the Kings		Egypt
Until They Sail		New Zealand
Never so Few		Ceylon, Thailand and Burma
Don't Go Near the Water		Hawaii

> In 1960 television began to take over in the entertainment business so I, like many others in my field, moved over to that area of employment.

As a Director of Photography, Voigtlander had over 500 television shows to his credit including series like "Ben Casey," "Bonanza," and "Little House on the Prairie." If you watched TV specials like "The Diary of Anne Frank," "The Miracle Worker," "Splendor in the Grass," or "The Loneliest Runner," Voigtlander did the photography.

Retired and living in Los Angeles, Voigtlander was a governor and member of the Board of the American Society of Cinematographers, a past governor of the National Academy of Television Arts & Sciences, and a member of the Motion Picture Academy. Two of his three children are involved in the entertainment business. Bill is a film editor at M.G.M. and UA and John is a writer and story analyst for Johnny Carson, Viacom and N.B.C. Voigtlander was inducted into the UI Hall of Fame in 1983. He died December 7, 1988 of cancer.

WALKER, Wayne   **1936-**   **Sandpoint**
                                                               Boise

Walker played professional football for the Detroit Lions from 1958-73, was selected All-Pro and played in the Pro Bowl in 1964, 1965, and 1966. He was born January 1, 1936 in Sandpoint and grew up in Boise. He came to UI from Boise, the same year Jerry Kramer arrived from Sandpoint, and played linebacker and center for four seasons, 1954-57. In his senior year he was captain of the Vandal team, was voted Most Valuable Player on defense in the East-West Shrine game and played in the College All-Star game in 1958. The fourth-round draft choice of the Detroit Lions, Walker played linebacker and place kicker for fifteen years, playing in 200 games. He missed only four games in his entire pro career.

In his sports column for the <u>Daily Idahonian</u> (January 21, 1988), on the occasion of the retirement of Walker's number 53 jersey, Harry Missildine wrote:

> A classmate of Jerry Kramer, Walker played for Skip Stahley's Vandals from 1954 through 1957. They were the principal teammates and principal destroyers of the East in the 1958 Shrine Game. Large, loose and rapid, Walker's one of those athletes of yesteryear who'd not merely succeed but excel in today's National Football League.
>
> At about 6'3" and 230 pounds, with smarts to go with his quickness and strength, Walker would be the model of a modern outside NFL linebacker, reacting effectively against runners or receivers. Walker played 15 seasons for the Detroit Lions, 1958 through 1973, made All-Pro five times, doubled as place kicker and became Detroit's No. 4 all-time scorer though he never kicked for the Idaho varsity.
>
> Walker's been a sports broadcaster and telecaster since his playing days, twice an Emmy winner as a CBS analyst; a former play-by-play man for the Oakland Athletics and now sports director for KPIX-TV in San Francisco.

Walker was selected in 1968 and 1971 as Idaho Male Athlete of the Year. His best year in pro football was 1964 when he scored 74 points (32 PATs and 14 FGs). Walker had fourteen career interceptions as a linebacker. He is a member of the Idaho Sports Hall of Fame.

According to <u>Idaho the University</u> magazine for summer 1988, which contains a feature article on Walker, only three other Vandal football players have had their jerseys retired. "... this mark of immortality" went to Ken Hobart ('84), John Yarno ('77), and Walker's illustrious teammate and friend, Jerry Kramer ('58).

WEYERHAEUSER, John Phillip, Jr.   1899-1956   Coeur d'Alene, Lewiston

He was President, Weyerhaeuser Timber Co., and grandson of the "Lumber King," Frederick Weyerhaeuser. To start at the beginning ... Frederick Weyerhaeuser was born November 21, 1834 in Niedersaulheim, Germany and came to America in 1852, first to Pennsylvania, then Illinois and finally St. Paul, Minn. where he died April 4, 1914. The empire started when be bought a defunct lumberyard in Rock Island, Ill. Following the logs to their source, he learned firsthand how wooded areas were cruised, trees were felled and logs were scaled. He bought into operations at each step of the way, acquiring partners as he did so. In 1900 Weyerhaeuser and his Midwest investing partners purchased 900,000 acres of forest land in western Washington and formed the Weyerhaeuser Timber Co. presided over by Frederick Weyerhaeuser from offices in Tacoma where his children, grandchildren and great-grandchildren were reared. Before WWI the company expanded its forest holdings throughout the Pacific Northwest including Idaho. After his death, his eldest son John Phillip served as president until he died in 1935. John Phillip Weyerhaeuser was born in Coal Valley, Ill. November 4, 1858 and died May 16, 1935. His brother Frederick Edward Weyerhaeuser (1872-1945) served as president from 1934-1945. John Phillip, Jr. was born January 18, 1899 in Rock Island, Ill. He received a B.A. from Yale and married Helen Walker October 25, 1922. Children -- Ann, John Phillip III, George Hunt, and Elizabeth. "Phil" Weyerhaeuser held various jobs in the lumber industry from 1920-22 and was sales manager of the Edw. Rutledge Timber Co., 1922-24, in Coeur d'Alene and general manager of the Clearwater Timber Company in Lewiston, 1925-31. In 1931 these two companies merged with the Potlatch Lumber Co. to become the Potlatch Forests, Inc. (PFI) and Phil Weyerhaeuser became president, 1931-32. In 1933 he left Idaho for Tacoma to become the executive vice president of Weyerhaeuser until 1947 when he replaced Frederick E. Weyerhaeuser as president, an office he held until his death in 1956. Subsequent Weyerhaeuser presidents were:

    - his brother Frederick K. Weyerhaeuser, 1956-66
    - his son George Hunt Weyerhaeuser, 1966-date, now 62

His children were born while he and Helen lived in Idaho. While in Lewiston the family lived at 308 N. Prospect Ave. until the family home at 603 9th St. was finished in 1927. Phil Weyerhaeuser was very civic minded, a member of the Lewiston Elks, a leader in the re-organization of the Lewiston Golf Club overlooking the Snake River. As the first president of PFI in April 1925 he helped plan and build the new plant at Lewiston, the beginning of integrated forest products industry in the region, and called the "world's largest whitepine saw mill." It began cutting logs August 8, 1927. The family was in the national spotlight in 1936 when their son George (the current Weyerhaeuser president) was kidnapped at the age of nine from his Tacoma home and held for $200,000 ransom. Phil Weyerhaeuser paid the ransom, his son was released unharmed and the kidnappers were later captured and sentenced to long prison terms. Phil Weyerhaeuser died of cancer, December 8, 1956. Weyerhaeuser sales and assets are in the billions and the company ranks with Xerox, Ford, Mobil, and BankAmerica Corp.

WILLIAMS, Roger   **1925-**   **Pocatello**

Pianist, composer, arranger, Roger Williams was born in 1925 in Omaha, Nebraska. <u>Time</u> August 2, 1968 pictures him at a punching bag and the story starts as follows:

> While the prelims are on the champ goes through his warm-up routine. He flexes hands that have been strengthened by years of squeezing a hard rubber ball. He slips on the gloves for a fast workout on a punching bag. Using an old fighter's trick, he smears Vaseline around his eyebrows to keep perspiration out of his eyes. Then Roger Williams, amateur boxer and former welterweight champion of Idaho's Farragut Naval Training Station, steps onstage for his nightly bout with the piano.

Roger Williams was one of 423 V-12 Navy trainees who reported to the University of Idaho Southern Branch at Pocatello on July 1, 1943, quartered in Gravelly Hall. A history of the Navy V-12 program says that "music was a big factor on the Pocatello campus -- there was a Navy chorus, a Navy band, and the piano selections of a trainee, Louis Weertz, who later became famous as Roger Miller:/WILLIAMS."

Williams returned to ISU for a B.A. in music, then received an M.A. in music from Drake University and further schooling at Julliard in New York where he studied classics.

The son of a Lutheran minister, by age eight he had learned to play thirteen instruments by ear, but did not get serious about the piano until one of his teachers told him he would never be anything but a music teacher. "That's when I started practicing eight, ten hours a day," he says.

He "always had a tremendous desire to be famous." In the Navy Williams almost lost his right index finger when a gun breech slammed shut on it. In New York he and his wife existed for seven jobless months on spaghetti -- even after he won on "Arthur Godfrey's Talent Scouts" by "banging out a symphonic arrangement of 'I Got Rhythm.'"

In 1954, the president of Kapp records heard him play in Manhattan's Madison Hotel cocktail lounge and signed him to a contract that led to "Autumn Leaves," his first hit record. In 1968, after 14 years, his 52 albums had sold close to fifteen million copies, making him, at 43, not only the largest-selling pianist in modern recording history but also the largest-selling instrumentalist of any kind.

"Autumn Leaves" and "Ebb Tide" are his best, most famous recordings.

WILLIAMSON, Thames Ross   **1894-1983(?)**   **Genesee**

Genesee-born Thames Ross Williamson was a prolific novelist during the 1920s, 1930s, and 1940s. His biographical sketch in <u>Twentieth Century Authors</u> (1942) says:

> American novelist, was born (February 7, 1894) on an Indian reservation
> near Genesee, Idaho where his father, Benjamin Franklin Williamson, a
> former scout, was a trader ...and he is of mixed Welsh, Norwegian,
> French and Irish descent. Perhaps because of this, he is a natural linguist,
> who speaks ten languages fluently. He ran away from home at fourteen,
> was a tramp for a while, then shipped to Peru on a treasure hunt, and then
> on a whaler which he deserted off the coast of Alaska. He has been a railroad
> worker, a circus roustabout, a sheepherder in the Sierra Nevada Mountains,
> and a reporter in San Francisco. Somehow in the midst of all of this, he
> managed to graduate from high school in Spokane, Washington.

The biography goes on to relate that at 20 he became private secretary to the warden of the Iowa State Prison and there was encouraged to become a writer by a prisoner who criticized a story in the prison magazine, which Williamson edited.

Deciding he needed more education, Williamson got his B.S. (cum laude) from the University of Iowa and went to Harvard on a scholarship where he received his M.A. in 1918, in economics and sociology. He did all the work for a Ph.D. except take the examination.

In 1920-21, he was assistant professor of economics at Simmons and 1921-22, assistant professor of economics and sociology at Smith College. Williamson wrote a number of textbooks on sociology from 1922-26 and the income enabled him to quit teaching and begin his long-projected plan to write about American life in a series of novels.

> After three far from successful volumes of the series, he abandoned the
> idea. It was 1929 before, with <u>Hunky</u>, he found his true voice -- that of
> the primitive, inarticulate members of our society.

He published at least one novel a year and sometimes two or three mysteries or juvenile titles as well. Many of the novels were on the Book-of-the-Month Club lists. Williamson wrote under five known pseudonyms and during the twenties and thirties lived variously in New England, Canada, France, Mexico and Sweden. In 1942 he was living in Massachusetts. His first name was pronounced, not like the English river, but "with a lisp at the start and rest to rhyme with James."

ZIMMER, Norma   1923-   Larson

Lawrence Welk's Champagne Lady during the 1960s and 1970s and, singer with the Billy Graham Crusade for Christ, was Norma Zimmer of Larson. The jacket of her autobiography, <u>Norma</u>, says:

> Perhaps not all her viewers realize that the source of Norma's radiance is her ardent faith in God and her confidence in His loving care. In this book, Norma tells her own life story - a story of incredible hardships in her youth: extreme poverty, alcoholic parents, unhappy home. With the utmost candor and entirely without self-pity, she shares the ups and downs of her journey to stardom, with praise for God's faithfulness.

Norma Beatrice Larsen was born July 13, 1923 in her grandfather's log cabin at Larson, a defunct railhead near Mullan. She was the third and unwanted child of Pete Larsen and Katherine Lempi Lindroos. Her maternal grandparents had started a dairy farm near Mullan. Her father's career as a concert violinist ended with an accident to his hand in a Seattle shipyard where he was working. His bad temper, quarrelling and drinking cost him several jobs and he decided to return with his two children, Max and Katherine (Kay), and his expectant wife, in 1923 to work in the mines near Mullan. It was here Norma was born.

After a mine accident when Norma was two, the Larsens returned again to the coast and lived in Tacoma. They first lived in a tenement and then rented a "tar paper shack" with no running water or electricity and paper-thin walls. The children wore "cast-off clothes and cardboard shoes." She wrote: "The winter of 1932 was the hardest of my life. We suffered from hunger and malnutrition. Even the plain macaroni and salt ran out ... we had bread for Thanksgiving." Her father often drank heavily and was argumentative. Her mother drank heavily from the time Norma was ten and had become an alcoholic. In later years she overcame this.

Through all this Pete Larsen taught young Norma violin and singing. About 1938 Max, and later the two daughters, joined the choir of the University Christian Church of Seattle. The director was Lincoln High School music teacher Carl A. Pitzer who also directed the high school glee club. Because of her knowledge of the violin and singing, Pitzer put her in the first violin section of the senior orchestra and the glee club. He also offered her free lessons and she studied voice with him all through high school. Norma became a featured church soloist and sang in several Lincoln High School plays.

After graduation she began singing at weddings for $5, did housework, worked in a grocery store, clerked at the Bon Marche and worked as a timekeeper for the U.S. Army Engineers. On a trip to Victoria, B.C. she happened to sing on a ship and was noticed by a Hollywood agent - Joe Chandler - who suggested she come there for an audition. She did and was hired at NBC for $24 a show. Later she was hired to sing as a member of the Tailor Mades trio.

She married Randy Zimmer, whom she had met several years earlier on a skiing trip to Snoqualmie Pass, the day before the Allied Armies Invaded Normandy on June 6, 1944. She began singing with a quartet called the Girl Friends and her career began to take off as they sang on the Eddie Canter Show, the Jack Benny Show and for Phil Harris, Dinah Shore, Lucille Ball, Nelson Eddy, Edgar Bergen, Bing Crosby, Frank Sinatra and others.

Norma sang background music in dozens of movies, sang regularly on eight weekly radio programs and had done hundreds of commercials. In November 1959, Lawrence Welk called and asked her to appear on his show. She sang "Smoke Gets in Your Eyes" and he asked her back for another appearance. This went on week after week and fan mail began pouring in. On the New Year's Eve show Lawrence Welk surprised her by asking on camera if she would join his musical family. In 1962 he asked her officially to become the "Champagne Lady" replacing Alice Lon. Norma remained on the show until it ran its course in the early 1980s. In the mid-1960s she also began singing in the Billy Graham Crusades.

For many years Norma Zimmer and her husband spent vacations at Soap Lake, Wash. where they own an apartment complex formerly owned by her father.

Norma may be seen on Lawrence Welk show re-runs currently seen on many PBS stations.

ADDENDA

Following is a brief listing of people with Idaho connections who have also achieved some degree of fame. These are names suggested to me or found in doing research on the main group. Some of this information has not been verified. I have been told, facetiously, that I missed some important people like Helen of Troy, Genesee Williams, and Huckleberry Fenn (Troy, Genesee and Fenn are small towns in North Idaho). It should be pointed out that Hollywood star Frances Gumm (better known as Judy Garland) was born in Grand Rapids, Minnesota, not Pocatello. Because she sang "I was born in a trunk in the Princess Theater in Pocatello, Idaho" in the movie "A Star is Born," many people think she was.

ANDROS, Dee   UI head football coach who went on to coach at Oregon State and later became Athletic Director there.

ARNOLD, Kenneth   Idaho businessman, reportedly the first person to sight a UFO, while flying his plane near Mt. Rainier in 1947.

ARCHER, David   From Soda Springs. Played football for Iowa State University and quarterbacked the Atlanta Falcons. Now with Miami Dolphins.

BEERY, Wallace   Movie actor. Had a cabin at Island Park. Filmed some of his movies at McCall.

BIRD, Francis   Lives at Lake Pend Oreille. Invented a respirator and became a millionaire when he sold the patent rights to 3M Company.

BROEMLING, William (BRIMLEY, WILFORD)   Television star of "Our House," owns land in Idaho. Makes radio commercials about Idaho and TV commercials about Quaker Oats.

BOWLING, Robert T.   Invented Pres-to-logs (TM) while working for Clearwater Timber (now Potlatch Forests, Inc.).

BUCHER, Lloyd   An Idaho native who grew up at St. Joseph's Mission, near Lapwai, and Boystown; was the former Navy Commander of the USS Pueblo who, along with his crew, was taken captive in 1968 by the North Koreans, the first of a series of U.S. hostages.

CHAMBERS, Cliff   Left handed major league pitcher with Cubs, Pirates, and Cards, from 1948-53. Lives in Boise.

CHAMBERLAIN, Lawrence, H.	From Challis. Critically acclaimed writer on American Government. Taught at UI. Received Honorary LLD, 1959. Vice President of Columbia University 1962-67. Died January 28, 1989.
CHARTERS, Harry	From Melba, world champion rodeo bulldogger in 1959. 6'6" and 250 pounds.
COLLINS, Judy	Pop music star with hit records including "Both Sides Now," and "Send in the Clowns," lived for a time in Lapwai. Her father, Charles Collins, the blind pianist who starred in radio and TV programs on the West Coast and at Denver, was raised in Lewiston and graduated from UI in 1937.
DAVIS, Wm.E. (Bud)	Former President of I.S.U. the University of New Mexico and Chancellor of the Oregon State System of Higher Education, 1982-88.
DAVID, Donald Kirk	Born in Moscow, became vice president of Columbia University.
DAWSON, John	Hailey artist. Designed popular 1988 cats block of U.S. Commemorative stamps and the 1990 Idaho Centennial stamp.
DOBBS, Lou	Attended UI Law School. "Moneyline" anchor person on CNN.
DONALDSON, Jean Chalmers	Internationally known poetess from Moscow. Deceased.
FAGERBAKKE, Bill	UI grad (1979) plays the part of Dauber, a football player on the ABC television series "Coach."
FERGUSON, Eddie	World freestyle skiing champ, named "Hotdogger of the Year" in 1973 by Skiing Magazine. Raised in Boise.
FORD, Tennessee Ernie	Retired country western singer, actor - lives part of the year at Grandjean, near Stanley.
GIBSON, Edward (Hoot)	1892-1962. Movie and vaudeville actor, circus and rodeo performer -- worked around the Salmon River area as a cowboy.
HANSON, Orval	Born in Firth, August 3, 1926. B.A. UI in 1950. Served four terms in the Idaho House of Representatives, one as majority leader, and three terms in the U.S. House of Representatives from 1969-75.

HARRIMAN, E. Roland	Banker-brother of W. Averell, spent time at their 10,700 acre Railroad Ranch. Donated in 1963 to State of Idaho and now is Harriman State Park, in SE Idaho, near Island Park.
HARRIS, Eugene	Internationally famous jazz pianist. Lives in Boise and plays regularly at the Idanha Hotel there. Has had a number of successful tours of Europe and Japan. Formerly played with Lionel Hampton and the Ray Brown Trio. One of his albums nominated for a Grammy Award in 1989. Born Benton Harbor, Michigan, 1933.
HOGE, Merrill	ISU grad, plays pro football for the NFL Pittsburgh Steelers.
HOLT, Dubby	ISU grad, football coach, and Athletic Director; was the 1956 Olympic Boxing Coach.
JACKSON, Reggie	With 563 career homers and number six on the all-time list, baseball's "Mr. October," played with Kansas City farm club in Lewiston in 1966 before moving up to the majors. Also played for Oakland, the New York Yankees, and the California Angels in his twenty-year career in the majors, 1967-87.
KARA, Theodore (Ted)	From Rupert, captain of the 1936 U.S. Olympic boxing team. Entered UI in 1937 and never lost a college bout, winning 33 and one draw. First to win three straight NCAA boxing titles.
KEINHOLTZ, Edward/ Nancy	Artists from Hope. UI grads.
KNIEVEL, Evel	Motorcycle stunt performer from Butte who attempted to jump the Snake River near Twin Falls, by the Perrine Bridge, in 1974.
LEMLEY, Jack K.	Former M-K vice president and management consultant from Boise is the CEO Transmanche Link, the Anglo-French joint venture building the English Channel Tunnel.
LLOYD, Andrea	Moscow High School grad, played on 1988 gold medal-winning U.S. Olympic basketball team in Seoul, Korea.
MAGNUSON, Harry F.	Successful investor. From Wallace, ISU grad, worked for Hecla Mining Company before forming own company for property and land investments.
MAYNARD, Ken	1895-1973. Cowboy movie star. Worked as a cowboy around Salmon River area.

McCALL, Tom — 1913-83. Two-term moderate Republican Governor of Oregon. Worked as a reporter for the <u>Daily Idahonian</u> (Moscow) in the late 1930s.

McDONALD, Ray — 6'4", 250 pound All-American fullback at UI. Played there 1963-66. Graduated from Caldwell H.S. All-State in football and track. Played professionally for the Washington Redskins.

McINTOSH, Carl — ISU graduate, served as President of ISU, Long Beach State and Montana State University.

McKAY, Allison — TV commercial star and actress, from Boise.

MILLER, Helen — Author of over thirty novels and biographies for children. Also a school teacher. Lived in Twin Falls and McCall.

MILLER, Joaquin — Real name Cincinatus H. Miller. As Joaquin Miller became renowned as "The poet of the Sierras." Came through Idaho in a covered wagon with his family in 1852 and later returned in 1860s to the gold rush around Florence and wrote of his experiences in Idaho. Millersburg was named after him.

NYBORG, Keith Foote — Born in Ashton, March 4, 1930. Rancher. Served as Ambassador to Finland, 1981-86.

PEEBLES, John J. — 1921-86. Born in Nampa. UI grad ('47), worked as an engineer for Idaho State Bureau of Reclamation (1947), U.S. Bureau of Reclamation (1948-53), Idaho Dept. of Highways (1954-62) and designed many bridges. He taught Civil Engineering at UI (1963-72) and worked for M-K (1972-86). Authored many articles dealing with civil engineering and PNW history and built a detailed model of the steam shovel used to construct Lake Lowell. The model is on display in the Idaho State Historical Museum Boise. Had numerous interests including music and mastered oil painting, astronomy, historical surveying techniques and mountain climbing. He scaled Mounts Borah, Ranier, Whitney, Hood and many others throughout the U.S.

PHILPOTT, LaVerne — Lived in Caldwell and Boise. College of Idaho grad; pioneered in radar, television and other electronics.

PHINNEY, Archie   Nez Perce writer, Indian agent. Born September 4, 1902 in Culdesac. Recipient of the Indian Council Fire Achievement Award (1948) given annually to an Indian whose accomplishments are considered worthy of national recognition. First Nez Perce to receive this award. UI's Phinney Hall named after him. Died in 1949.

PITMAN, Doug   ISU grad. One of the founders of Boise-based Micron Technology Inc., along with twins Ward and Joseph Parkinson.

SALZER, Jerry   Born October 9, 1939 in Nampa. B.S., M.S. and Sc.D. from MIT. Joined IBM in 1970 and the faculty at MIT in 1976. Cited in 1983 by the Institute of Electrical and Electronic Engineers for his "contributions to design of large-scale computer operating systems."

SCHROM, Ken   Born November 13, 1954 in Grangeville. Played football and baseball at UI, 1974-76. Played major league baseball as a pitcher for the Toronto Blue Jays, Minnesota Twins, and Cleveland Indians. Selected for the All-Star game in 1986.

SEUBERT, Jean   1964 Olympic skier from McCall.

SKAGGS, Marion Barton   In 1926, consolidated his food and drug stores with a California group and started Safeway food store chain. Began with a small grocery store in American Falls in 1915.

SOUTHERN, Ann   Movie actress during 1940s and 1950s. Star of "Private Secretary" television series. Had a place at Hayden Lake and has a home at Sun Valley. Her sister, Sally, lives in Boise.

STEARNS, H. Myrl   UI grad, 1937. President of Varian Associates.

TAYLOR, Glen   U.S. Senator from Idaho. Ran for vice president in 1948 on Progressive Party ticket with Henry Wallace. Grew up in Kooskia.

TEATER, Archie Boyd   Born May 5, 1901 in Boise, studied art in Portland and N.Y.C. Gained world-wide reputation for landscapes, especially mountain views -- Grand Tetons, etc. Spent a large part of his career in the Hagerman Valley, near Bliss in a studio home designed by Frank Lloyd Wright called Teater's Knoll which projects over a cliff high above the Snake River. Died July 19, 1978 in Rochester, Minnesota.

WALTON, Anita

Silent screen actress born in Boise. Maiden name Lieberman. Boise H.S. grad. Made pictures for D.W. Griffith at Universal Studios.

WERNER, Louis B.

Helped isolate chemical elements curium and plutonium. From Nampa.

WEST, James F.

Real estate developer, philanthropist, and cattle rancher. Attended UI in 1930s. Founder of Riverside International Raceway in California. Owned a number of restaurants and cattle ranches. Returned to live in Idaho in 1978. Died at Sun Valley, 1987.

WILLIE, Boxcar

Worked for KGEM radio in Boise.

YARNO, John

UI All-American football center in mid-1970s. Played professionally with Denver and Seattle Seahawks.

ZOBELL, Claude

ISU grad. Considered the Father of Marine Biology.

This is a very abbreviated list. There seems to be no end to the number of Famous Idahoans. Idaho also had some infamous folks but that's another story.

SELECTED REFERENCES

Most of the individuals listed in this book who are still living may be found in <u>Who's Who in America</u>, Chicago, Ill. A.N. Marquis. Many of the deceased persons are listed in <u>Who Was Who in America</u>, Chicago, Ill. A. N. Marquis Co. Those of historical importance may be found in general encyclopedias.

Some current information has been taken from newspapers and citations to them have been made in the articles themselves. Many of the articles cited and most of the books have bibliographies of their own. Some of the more common references include:

BOOKS, ENCYCLOPEDIAS, ETC.

    Beal, Merrill and Wells, Merle. <u>History of Idaho</u>, N.Y. Lewis Historical Publishing Co., 1959.
    <u>Contemporary Authors</u>. Detroit, Mich. Gale Research Co., 1981.
    <u>Current Biography</u>. N.Y., H.W. Wilson Co., 1940-date.
    Gibbs, Rafe. <u>Beckoning the Bold</u>, Moscow, Idaho, University Press of Idaho. 1976.
    <u>Idaho Encyclopedia</u>. Caldwell, Idaho, Caxton Printers, LTD. 1938.
    <u>Reader's Encyclopedia of the American West</u>, N.Y., Crowell. 1977.
    <u>Twentieth Century Authors</u>. N.Y., H.W. Wilson Co. 1942.
    Wells, Merle and Hart, Arthur. <u>Idaho: Gem of the Mountains</u>. Northridge, CA. Windsor Publications, Inc., 1985.
    <u>Who's Who in the West</u>. Chicago, Ill. A. N. Marquis.
    Young, Virgil. <u>The Story of Idaho</u>, Moscow, Idaho. University Press of Idaho, 2nd ed. 1984.

NEWSPAPERS

    <u>The Argonaut</u>. Moscow, Idaho. University of Idaho.
    <u>Daily Idahonian</u>. Moscow, Idaho.
    <u>Idaho Statesman</u>. Boise, Idaho.
    <u>Lewiston Tribune</u>. Lewiston, Idaho.

PERIODICALS

    <u>The Bookmark</u>. Moscow, Idaho. University of Idaho. The Library.
    <u>Cold-Drill (Extra)</u>. Boise, Idaho. Boise State University. 1984.
    <u>Newsweek</u>, New York, N.Y. Newsweek, Inc.
    <u>Time</u>, New York, N.Y. Time, Inc.

****

AGEE <u>Lewiston Tribune</u>, Lewiston, Idaho. August 5-6, 1988.
<u>USA Today</u>, Washington, D.C., Gannett.
  September 2, 1988.
<u>Who's Who in America</u>, Chicago, Ill. A.N. Marquis,
  1987.

ALBERTSON <u>Supermarket News</u>. N.Y., Fairchild Publications,
  Inc. August 18, 1969.
<u>Idaho Statesman</u>. Boise, Idaho. April 18, 1976,
  May 26, 1977, July 28, 1978, etc.
Wells, Merle. <u>Idaho: Gem of the Mountains</u>.
  Northridge, CA. Windsor. 1985.

ALEXANDER Crowder, David. <u>Tales of Eastern Idaho</u>. Idaho
  Falls, Idaho. KID Broadcasting Co., 1981.
Gibbs, Rafe. <u>Beckoning the Bold</u>. Moscow, University Press of Idaho, 1976.

ANDRUS <u>Current Biography</u>. N.Y., H.W. Wilson Co., 1977.

ANGLETON <u>Time</u>. New York, N.Y. Time, Inc. January 6, 1975.
<u>Newsweek</u>. New York, N.Y. Newsweek, Inc. January
  6, 1975.
<u>Political Profiles</u>. N.Y., Facts on File, Inc., 1979.

BELL <u>The Argonaut</u>, Moscow, Idaho. University of Idaho.
<u>Current Biography</u>, N.Y., H.W. Wilson Co., 1976.
U.S. Congress. Senate Committee on Labor and
  Human Resources. <u>Hearing</u>. Washington, D.C.
  U.S. G.P.O., January 15, 1981.

BEMIS Gibbs, Rafe. <u>Beckoning the Bold</u>. Moscow, Idaho.
  University Press of Idaho, 1976.

BENSON <u>Current Biography</u>. N.Y., H.W. Wilson Co., 1953.

BLAKLEY ASCAP. <u>Biographical Dictionary</u>. N.Y., Jacques
  Cattell Press, 1980.
<u>Illustrated Who's Who of the Cinema</u>. N.Y.,
  MacMillan, 1983.
<u>Motion Picture Guide</u>. Chicago, Ill. Cinebooks,
  Inc., 1985.

BOLLINGER <u>The Argonaut</u>, Moscow, Idaho. University of Idaho,
  November 2, 1944.
<u>Lewiston Tribune</u>. Lewiston, Idaho. July 12, 1962.

BORAH <u>Current Biography</u>. N.Y., H.W. Wilson Co., 1940.
<u>Daily Idahonian</u>. Moscow, Idaho. March 26-27, 1988.

BORGLUM   The Bookmark. Moscow, Idaho. University of Idaho.
         The Library. Fall, 1984.
         Current Biography. N.Y., H.W. Wilson Co., 1941.
         Crowder, David. Tales of Eastern Idaho. Idaho
             Falls, Idaho. KID Broadcasting Co., 1981.
         Mount Rushmore Voice. Mount Rushmore, S.D. U.S.
             Park Service. Summer, 1988.

BOYINGTON   Spokesman-Review. Spokane, Washington, January
             12, 1988.
         Time. N.Y. Time, Inc., January 10, 1944, January
             17, 1944, April 24, 1944, September 2, 1946.
         Life, Chicago, Ill. Time, Inc., October 1, 1945.

BRINK   The Bookmark. Moscow, Idaho. University of Idaho.
         The Library, Fall, 1984.
         Current Biography. N.Y., H.W. Wilson Co., 1946.
         Cold-Drill (Extra). Boise, Idaho. Boise State
             University. 1984.
         Who's Who Among Pacific Northwest Authors. PNLA
             1970.
         Contemporary Authors. Detroit, Mich. Gale Research
             Co., 1967.

BROOKS, M.   New York Times. New York, N.Y., February 17, 1977.
         Who's Who of American Women. Chicago, Ill. A. N.
             Marquis. 1974/75.

BROOKS, P.   Cold-Drill (Extra). Boise, Idaho. Boise State
             University, 1984.
         Halliwell's Filmgoers Companion. N.Y., Scribners.
             8th Ed., 1985.

BURROUGHS   Academic American Encyclopedia. Danbury, Conn.
             Grolier Inc., 1984.
         Porges, Irwin. Edgar Rice Burroughs, the Man
             Who Created Tarzan. Provo, Utah. BYU Press,
             1975.

CATALDO, Fr.   Reader's Encyclopedia of the American West. N.Y.
             Crowell, 1977.

CHURCH   Current Biography. N.Y., H.W. Wilson Co., 1978,
             1984.
         Idaho Blue Book. Boise, Idaho. State of Idaho,
             1969/70.

COBB   Academic American Encyclopedia. Danbury, Conn.
             Grolier Inc., 1984.
         Current Biography. N.Y., H.W. Wilson Co., 1951.

DAVIS   University of Idaho, Moscow, Idaho. Alumni
             Office.
         Idaho, the University. Moscow, Idaho. University
             of Idaho, Fall, 1987.

DISNEY   <u>Current Biography</u>. N.Y., H.W. Wilson Co., 1952.
                  Mosley, Leonard. <u>Disney's World</u>. N.Y. Stein
                      & Day, 1985.

DUBOIS   <u>Reader's Encyclopedia of the American West</u>. N.Y.
                      Crowell, 1977.
                  Gibbs, Rafe. <u>Beacon for Mountain and Plain</u>.
                      Moscow, Idaho. University of Idaho, 1962.
                  Gibbs, Rafe. <u>Beckoning the Bold</u>. Moscow, Idaho.
                      University Press of Idaho, 1976.

EARP   <u>Academic American Encyclopedia</u>. Danbury, Conn.
                      Grolier Inc., 1984.
                  <u>The Bookmark</u>. Moscow, Idaho. University of Idaho.
                      The Library, December 1959.
                  Gibbs, Rafe. <u>Beckoning the Bold</u>. Moscow, Idaho.
                      University Press of Idaho. 1976.
                  <u>Reader's Encyclopedia of the American West</u>. N.Y.,
                      Crowell, 1977.

EDMUNDSON   <u>The Bookmark</u>. Moscow, Idaho. University of Idaho.
                      The Library, Fall, 1984.
                  Gibbs, Rafe. <u>Beacon for Mountain and Plain</u>.
                      Moscow, Idaho. University of Idaho, 1962.

ELSENSOHN   <u>Who's Who Among Pacific Northwest Authors</u>. PNLA.
                      1957.

ENGLEHORN   Alliss, Peter. <u>The Who's Who of Golf</u>. Englewood
                      Cliffs, N.J. Prentice-Hall, 1983.
                  <u>Sports Illustrated</u>. N.Y., Time, Inc., June 29, 1970.

FARLEY   Promotional material supplied from Eric Semon
                      Associates, New York, N.Y.
                  <u>Who's Who in America</u>. Chicago, Ill. A. N. Marquis,
                      1988.

FARNSWORTH   <u>National Inventors Hall of Fame</u>. Washington, D.C.,
                      U.S. Department of Commerce, 1987.
                  Young, Virgil. <u>The Story of Idaho</u>. Moscow, Idaho.
                      University Press of Idaho. 2nd ed. 1984.

FERY   Wells, Merle. <u>Idaho: Gem of the Mountains</u>.
                      Northridge, CA. Windsor Publications, 1985.
                  <u>Idaho Statesman</u>. Boise, Idaho. April 31, 1977,
                      October 21, 1979, etc.

FISHER   <u>American Academic Encyclopedia</u>. Danbury, Conn.
                      Grolier Inc., 1984.
                  <u>Twentieth Century Authors</u>. N.Y., H.W. Wilson Co.,
                      1942.

FOOTE <u>American Women Writers</u>. N.Y., Frederick Ungar, 1979.
<u>Cold-Drill (Extra)</u>. Boise, Idaho, Boise State University, 1984.

FRENCH <u>The Bookmark</u>. Moscow, Idaho. University of Idaho. The Library, 1970.
<u>Daily Idahonian</u>. Moscow, Idaho. July 4, 1987.

GALLOWAY University of Idaho. Moscow, Idaho. Alumni Office.

GHORMLEY <u>Daily Idahonian</u>. Moscow, Idaho. July 4, 1987.
Gibbs, Rafe. <u>Beacon for Mountain and Plain</u>. Moscow, Idaho. University of Idaho, 1962.

GILBERT <u>The Bookmark</u>. Moscow, Idaho. University of Idaho. The Library, Fall, 1984.
<u>Daily Idahonian</u>. Moscow, Idaho. July 4, 1987.

GIPSON <u>Current Biography</u>. N.Y., H.W. Wilson Co., 1954, 1971

GOFF <u>Daily Idahonian</u>. Moscow, Idaho. July 4, 1987.
University of Idaho. The Library. Special Collections. Goff Papers.

HABIB <u>Current Biography</u>. N.Y., H.W. Wilson Co., 1981.

HARRIMAN <u>Current Biography</u>. N.Y., H.W. Wilson Co., 1946.
Wells, Merle. <u>Idaho: Gem of the Mountains</u>. Northridge, CA. Windsor. 1985.
<u>Time</u>. N.Y., Time Inc., August 4, 1986.
Young, Virgil. <u>The Story of Idaho</u>. Moscow, Idaho. University Press of Idaho, 2nd ed., 1984.

HEMINGWAY (Ernest) <u>Academic American Encyclopedia</u>. Danbury, Conn. Grolier, 1984.

HEMINGWAY (Margaux/ Mariel) <u>Cold-Drill (Extra)</u>. Boise, Idaho. Boise State University. 1984.
<u>Current Biography</u>. N.Y., H.W. Wilson Co., 1978.
<u>Time</u>. N.Y. Time Inc. June 16, 1975.
<u>Newsweek</u>. N.J. Newsweek Inc., March 17, 1975.

HOBART University of Idaho. Moscow, Idaho. Sports Information Office.

HURDSTROM <u>The Argonaut</u>. Moscow, Idaho. University of Idaho. October 12, 15, 1965.

JACKSON <u>The Baseball Encyclopedia</u>. N.Y., MacMillan, 1976.
<u>Lewiston Tribune</u>. Lewiston, Idaho. August 19, 30, 1987.

JENNINGS
The Bookmark. Moscow, Idaho. University of Idaho.
The Library, Fall, 1985.
Cold-Drill (Extra). Boise, Idaho. Boise State
University, 1984.

JEWETT
Beal, Merill. History of Idaho. N.Y., Lewis
Historical Publishing Co., 1959.

JOHNSON, G.
Lewiston Tribune. Lewiston, Idaho. March 21, 1987
Idaho the University. Moscow, Idaho. University of
Idaho, Fall, 1987.

JOHNSON, W.
The Baseball Encyclopedia. N.Y., MacMillan, 1976.
Hickok, Ralph.
Who Was Who in American Sports.
N.Y., Hawthorne Books, Inc., 1971.

JOHNSTON
American Men and Women of Science. N.Y., Bowker,
Inc, 1986.
The Argonaut. Moscow, Idaho. University of Idaho.
September 20, 1983.
Daily Idahonian. Moscow, Idaho. May 21-22, 1988.
Newsweek. NYC. Newsweek, Inc. July 28, 1985.

JORDAN
Beal, Merrill. History of Idaho. N.Y., Lewis
Historical Publishing Co., 1959.
Idaho Blue Book. Boise, Idaho. State of Idaho,
1969/70.

JOSEPH
Academic American Encyclopedia. Danbury, Conn.
Grolier Inc., 1984.
Gibbs, Rafe. Beckoning the Bold. Moscow, Idaho.
University Press of Idaho, 1972.

JUVE
The Bookmark. Moscow, Idaho. University of Idaho.
The Library, Fall, 1984.
Daily Idahonian. Moscow, Idaho. June 5, 1984.
Moskowitz, Sam. "Henrik Dahl Juve and the Second
Gernsback Dynasty." Extrapolation. Kent State
University Press. Spring, 1989.

KILLEBREW
Current Biography. N.Y., H.W. Wilson Co., 1966.

KING
Current Biography. N.Y., H.W. Wilson Co., 1974.
Baker's Biographical Dictionary of Musicians.
N.Y. Schirmer Books, 7th Ed., 1984.
Rolling Stone Encyclopedia of Rock and Roll.
Rolling Stone Press/Summit Books, 1983.

KRAMER
Biographical Dictionary of American Sports-
Football. ed. by David L. Porter. N.Y.,
Greenwood Press. 1987.

LAW
Current Biography. N.Y., H.W. Wilson, 1961.

LAWYER   Beal, Merrill. _History of Idaho_. N.Y., Lewis
                Historical Publishing Co., 1959.
            Gibbs, Rafe. _Beckoning the Bold_. Moscow, Idaho.
                University Press of Idaho, 1976.
            Young, Virgil. _The Story of Idaho_. Moscow,
                Idaho. University Press of Idaho. 2nd Ed.,
                1984.

LIND   Information sent by family.

LINDLEY   _Current Biography_. N.Y., H.W. Wilson Co., 1943.

LYNN   _Cold-Drill (Extra)_. Boise, Idaho. Boise State
                University. 1984.
            The Country Music Encyclopedia. N.Y., Crowell, 1974.

MAXEY   _Contemporary Authors_. Detroit, Mich. Gale
                Research Co., 1981.

McCLURE   _Idaho Blue Book_. Boise, Idaho. State of Idaho,
                1969/70.
            Who's Who in American Politics, 1987/88. N.Y.,
                Bowker Co., 11th Ed., 1987.

McCONNELL   Otness, Lillian. _A Great Good Country_. Moscow,
                Idaho. Latah County Historical Society, 1983.
            Daily Idahonian. Moscow, Idaho. July 4, 1987.

McKENNA   _Cold-Drill (Extra)_. Boise, Idaho. Boise State
                University, 1984.
            Contemporary Authors. Detroit, Mich. Gale Research
                Co., 1981.
            Motion Picture Guide. Chicago, Ill. Cinebooks,
                Inc., 1985.

McMANUS   _Contemporary Authors_. Detroit, Mich. Gale Research
                Co., 1981.
            Lewiston Tribune. Lewiston, Idaho. November 20,
                1987.

MILLER   _Idaho the University_. Moscow, Idaho. University of
                Idaho. September, 1985.
            Los Angeles Times. Los Angeles, California.
                April 16, 1987.

MORGAN   _Central Idaho_. Grangeville, Idaho. Mark and Lori
                Wilkens. Summer, 1987.

MORRISON   Beal, Merrill. _History of Idaho_. N.Y., Lewis
                Historical Publishing Co., 1959.
            Gibbs, Rafe. _Beckoning the Bold_. Moscow, Idaho.
                University Press of Idaho, 1976.
            Young, Virgil. _The Story of Idaho_. Moscow, Idaho
                University Press of Idaho, 1984.

O'CONNOR   <u>Who's Whom Among Pacific Northwest Authors</u>. PNLA, 1970.

OLIVER   <u>Saturday Evening Post</u>. Philadelphia, PA Curtis, December 2, 1961.

POUND   <u>Academic American Encyclopedia</u>. Danbury, Conn. Grolier, Inc., 1984.

REINHARDT   <u>Current Biography</u>. N.Y., H.W. Wilson, 1941.
<u>Time</u>. N.Y., Time Inc., June 3, 1940.

RENFREW   <u>Who's Who in the West</u>. Chicago, Ill. A. N. Marquis, 1988.

REVERE   Stambler, Irwin. <u>Encyclopedia of Pop, Rock and Soul</u>. N.Y. St. Martins Press, 1974.

REYNOLDS   <u>Cold-Drill (Extra)</u>. Boise, Idaho. Boise State University, 1984.
<u>Colliers</u>. Springfield, Ohio. Crowell-Collier, November 7, 1942.
<u>Motion Picture Guide</u>. Chicago, Ill. Cinebooks, Inc., 1985.

ROBB   <u>Cold-Drill (Extra)</u>. Boise, Idaho. Boise State University, 1984.
<u>Current Biography</u>. N.Y., H.W. Wilson, 1958.

ROBERTSON   <u>Idaho Encyclopedia</u>. Caldwell, Idaho. Caxton Printers, LTD. 1938.
<u>Who's Who Among Pacific Northwest Authors</u>. PNLA, 1957.
<u>Daily Idahonian</u>. Moscow, Idaho, July 4, 1987.

ROBINSON   Beal, Merrill. <u>History of Idaho</u>. N.Y., Lewis Historical Publishing Co., 1959.
<u>Daily Idahonian</u>. Moscow, Idaho, January 23, 1980, July 4, 1987.

ROMNEY   <u>Current Biography</u>. N.Y., H. W. Wilson Co., 1958.
<u>Encyclopedia Americana</u>. Danbury, Conn. Grolier Inc., 1984.

SACAJAWEA   <u>Reader's Encyclopedia of the American West</u>. N.Y., Crowell, 1977.
Crowder, David. <u>Tales of Eastern Idaho</u>. Idaho Falls, Idaho. KID Broadcasting Co., 1981.
Waldo, Anna Lee. <u>Sacajawea</u>. New York, N.Y. Avon Books, 1978.

SARETT   <u>National Inventors Hall of Fame</u>. Washington, D.C. U.S. Department of Commerce, 1987.

SHRONTZ   <u>Who's Who in the West</u>. Chicago, Ill. A. N. Marquis
            1988.

SIMPLOT   Beal, Merrill. <u>History of Idaho</u>. N.Y., Lewis
            Historical Publishing Co., 1959.
            Wells, Merle. <u>Idaho: Gem of the Mountains</u>.
            Northridge, CA. Windsor Publications Inc.,
            1985.
            Young, Virgil. <u>The Story of Idaho</u>. Moscow, Idaho.
            University Press of Idaho, 2nd Ed., 1984.
            <u>Idaho Statesman</u>. Boise, Idaho, May 9, 1982.

SMITH, E   <u>The Argonaut</u>. Moscow, Idaho. University of Idaho.
            October 31, 1980. October 7, 1983.
            <u>The Bookmark</u>. Moscow, Idaho. University of Idaho.
            The Library, Fall, 1984.
            <u>Twentieth Century Science Fiction Writers</u>. N.Y.,
            St. Martins Press, 1981.

SMITH, P   <u>Cold-Drill (Extra)</u>. Boise, Idaho. Boise State
            University, 1984.

SORRELS   <u>Encyclopedia of Folk, Country and Western Music</u>.
            N.Y., St. Martin's Press, 1983.
            <u>Daily Idahonian</u>. Moscow, Idaho. July 19, 1986,
            September 18, 1987.
            <u>Idaho Statesman</u>. Boise, Idaho. January 27, 1985,
            December 8, 1985.

SPALDING   <u>Reader's Encyclopedia of the American West</u>. N.Y.,
            Crowell, 1977.
            Young, Virgil. <u>The Story of Idaho</u>. Moscow, Idaho.
            University Press of Idaho, 2nd Ed., 1984.

STEINMAN   <u>The Bookmark</u>. Moscow, Idaho. University of Idaho.
            The Library, September 1963, Fall, 1984.
            <u>Current Biography</u>. N.Y., H.W. Wilson Co., 1957.
            <u>Daily Idahonian</u>. Moscow, Idaho, July 4, 1987.
            <u>McGraw Hill Modern Scientists and Engineers</u>. V.3.
            New York, McGraw Hill. 1980.

TRUEBLOOD   <u>Who's Who Among Pacific Northwest Authors</u>. PNLA.
            1970.
            <u>Idaho Statesman</u>. Boise, Idaho. September 14-15,
            19, 1982.

TURNER   <u>Cold-Drill (Extra)</u>. Boise, Idaho. Boise State
            University, 1984.
            <u>Current Biography</u>. N.Y., H.W. Wilson Co., 1943.
            Thompson, David. <u>Biographical Dictionary of Film</u>.
            N.Y., Morrow, 1981.
            Turner, Lana. <u>Lana - the Lady, the Legend, the</u>
            <u>Truth</u>. N.Y., Dutton, 1982.

VOIGTLANDER   Voigtlander, Ted. Letter to University of Idaho.
        Alumni Relations, February 18, 1983.

WALKER   <u>Idaho the University</u>. Moscow, Idaho. University
        of Idaho, Summer, 1988.
     <u>Daily Idahonian</u>. Moscow, Idaho, January 21, 23,
        24, 1988.

WEYERHAEUSER   <u>Current Biography</u>. N.Y., H.W. Wilson Co., 1977.
     <u>Lewiston Tribune</u>. Lewiston, Idaho. December 5,
        1956.
     Twining, Charles E. <u>Phil Weyerhaeuser, Lumberman</u>.
        Seattle, University of Washington Press, 1985.

WILLIAMS   ASCAP <u>Biographical Dictionary</u>. N.Y. Jacques Cattell
        Press, 1980.
     <u>Time</u>. N.Y., Time, Inc., August 2, 1968.

WILLIAMSON   <u>Twentieth Century Authors</u>. N.Y., H.W. Wilson Co.,
        1942.

ZIMMER   Zimmer, Norma. <u>Norma</u>. N.Y., Wheaton, Ill.
        Tyndale House, 1976.